Put down your phone

Be less busy and be more awesome

Let's live in a world with more high fives

If it doesn't make the world better, don't do it

LOOK FOR WHAT MATTERS   As human beings, we are capable of lots of bad stuff, but also cupcakes

COMPLAIN LESS. CELEBRATE MORE.

Every time you see a slide, go down it

Sing out loud. You don't have to have a reason to.

LAUGH!

Treat everybody like it's their birthday

HELP END GLOBAL SADNESS.

TAKE ... **AX.**

BR...

PICTURES

...T SWEAT THE SMALL STUFF. Life is short, and deodorant is expensive.

Bring awesome back

FOCUS ON THE AWESOME

GET OUT THERE!

FOLLOW YOUR PASSION

MAIL YOUR FRIEND A CORNDOG

Every room you enter? FREE HUGS!

If you see spinach (or anything else) in somebody's teeth, tell them, but only after you've told them something embarrassing about yourself

HAVE A PIZZA DELIVERED TO SOMEONE YOU DISAGREE WITH

We need to live in a world with fewer selfies and more otherpeoplies

Practice the art of the unexpected burrito!

RECOGNIZE REAL BEAUTY

Two words: "Share"

Celebrate somebody's birthday by celebrating other people

Sacrifice. Let someone else have the toy in the cereal.

Be somebody who makes everybody feel like a somebody

TALK GOODER! Listen (more than you talk) ASK QUESTIONS

STAND IN SOMEONE ELSE'S SHOES (METAPHORICALLY)

Leave notes complimenting people on how well they parked

CONNECT WITH PEOPLE!

ASK PEOPLE IF THEY REMEMBER BEING A KID   Make laughter your official language

If you want to be a world changer for people everywhere, be a day maker for the people right next to you

SEND A CARD. EVERY DAY. FOR 365 DAYS. BE CONFIDENT. It's contagious.

Be cool to people even if they're not cool to you, because somebody was probably not cool to them

Find your light (and share it)

Paint a park bench   Ask your best friend for help   INVENT A NEW HANDSHAKE

SOLVE A CONFLICT USING ICE CREAM!   BE FRUITFUL   Tip Big, Yo

HIGH FIVE YOUR DENTIST

DECLARE AN ENTIRE MONTH SOMETHING AWESOME   WRITE LETTERS

THINK MORE LIKE A KID

Write and record a song for someone

THINK OF SOMETHING YOU WANT TO SAY, AND THEN SING IT INSTEAD

READ. THEN READ SOME MORE.

Help somebody WHO IS YOUNGER THAN YOU

Don't be in a party.

Love changes everything, so fill the world with it

BE A PARTY.

THROW A PARADE!

THROW A POP-UP ART SHOW

BE LIKE CHEESE (OR BACON) AND MAKE EVERYTHING YOU TOUCH BETTER

TAKE SOMEONE'S PHOTO AND HAND-DELIVER IT TO THEM

give the world a reason to dance

PUT TAPE ON YOUR NOSE. IT'S A GREAT CONVERSATION STARTER.

COME UP WITH NAMES FOR THINGS THAT ALREADY HAVE NAMES

Meow the words to your favorite songs. We call this cat caroling.

BEHOLD THE POWER OF POSITIVE PARTYING

spread confetti (the Earth-friendly kind)!

Be kind. It's not always easy, but it's always important.

WRITE A POEM

GATHER YOUR FRIENDS, DRESS UP LIKE SUPERHEROES, AND DO SOMEONE'S YARD WORK

for somebody who doesn't normally get poems written about them

Wear something awesome

Invent a Dance

JOIN A MOVEMENT

USE YOUR IMAGINATION!

START WITH YOUR HEART... AND THEN JUST START

Be Generous. Give!

START SIMPLE

MAKE SOMETHING AWESOME!

BROADCAST the good news around you!

Spend time with your family!

Do what you like, and share it with others

Give out handmade awards

LICK THE WALLS OF THE WHITE HOUSE

TAKE A MOMENT TO REFLECT

KISS BEYONCÉ

HELP SOMEONE PROPOSE

LET YOUR HEROES KNOW THEY ARE YOUR HEROES

Teachers keep teaching. Students keep studenting.

IT'S OKAY TO GET DISCOURAGED...

REMEMBER: THINGS DON'T HAVE TO BE THE WAY THEY ARE

Don't get tired. Get inspired.

TAKE CARE OF YOURSELF, SO YOU CAN TAKE CARE OF OTHERS

Change the future

Write down your dreams

TEAM UP! TOGETHER, WE'RE LOUDER

REMEMBER THAT THE WORLD IS BIGGER THAN YOUR BACKYARD

LOOK BACKWARDS AND FORWARDS

DREAM BIGGER

start writing on a page and then lose track of...

KID PRESIDENT'S
GUIDE TO BEING
AWESOME

BY
BRAD MONTAGUE &
ROBBY NOVAK

HARPER
An Imprint of HarperCollinsPublishers

ISBN 978-0-06-243871-3

Photographs: Kristi Montague (unless otherwise noted)
Layout: Russell Shaw (unless otherwise noted)
Additional photography and design credits and copyrights noted on pages
252–253. All fan photos and user-generated images were submitted to Kid
President and SoulPancake and are used herein with permissions.
16 17 18 19 20 PC/RRDW 10 9 8 7 6 5 4 3 2
First paperback edition, 2016

CONTENTS

the Search for Joy

Or, Why It's Always a Good Idea to Have a Guy from Tennessee on Your Team

Preface by Rainn Wilson

How is it that the most dynamic, ridiculous, inspiring, charming, silly kid who ever wore a cheap suit and inhabited a Tiny Oval Office came to be the biggest internet sensation since the piano-playing cat? Simple. Because myself and the good folks at SoulPancake undertook a search for joy.

When I used to tell people why I started SoulPancake—to spark a dialogue about art and philosophy, spirituality and creativity—people would nod politely (I am, after all, incredibly famous and insanely handsome) and then immediately harbor secret thoughts that I might be slightly insane.

Today, I tell people SoulPancake exists to help spread joy and make the world a better place. I get a much better response.

Creating joyful content was always important to us, but not always our first priority. We had a creative website and bestselling book; we'd made some pretty terrific, vibrant videos for the Oprah Winfrey Network. So when we launched our premium YouTube channel back in July 2012, we decided to stay the course—create challenging, meaningful content that touched the heart as well as the mind.

We did everything we could at first to drum up subscribers—I have personally given piggyback rides to senior citizens, meditated in a Speedo, and toilet-papered Elijah Wood's house. In those early days of our channel's launch, our team was exhausted. Some had taken to sleeping under sound blankets; others were stockpiling sugar-free Red Bull in the corner of our makeshift conference room. But our content was coming together. We were telling great stories! We had existential interviews with famous people! Surprisingly touching profiles of the homeless! Inspiring documentaries about the terminally ill!

But about 3 weeks into this giant online content incubation experiment, despite having about 150,000 subscribers, we realized something: Our compelling, inspiring content was feeling a bit too, well, heavy.

So we called a meeting.

My friend and SoulPancake co-founder Devon proclaimed: "You know what? We need more joy on the channel!"

That was it! Joy is universal. It's human. It connects us. And moves us. We needed joy! The words were said. We had projected them into the universe. There was just one problem: We didn't know where to go to find it!

Little did we know that in a Tennessee town with a population of about 6,500 people, that spark of joy was already being cultivated.

Within days of issuing our joy mandate, a grainy video featuring a little boy wearing a tiny suit, standing in front of a cardboard set came across our desks. The first words we ever heard the exuberant Robby Novak say to us were: "People of the internet! Get off your Facebook, and listen to me! If it doesn't make the world better, don't do it!"

We sat up and paid attention. Could this be? Joy incarnate? From a town most famous for its annual whole-hog barbecue festival?

Within days, we reached out with an offer to help promote and feature this "Kid President" and partner up with the kind, brilliant man behind the videos, Robby's brother-in-law, Brad Montague. Brad was hesitant—he told us he wasn't even sure he wanted to make more than the handful of videos he and Robby had already created. He had no idea who we were or what this "SoulPancake" was about.

But Devon, who happens to be from Nashville, picked up the phone and called Brad, using all of his wacky, backwoods Tennessee charm. Virtual hands were shaken, and Kid President joined up with the SoulPancake team a few days later.

I'd like to think that Brad and Robby came to work with SoulPancake because they believed in our vision to create inspiring work that explores "Life's Big Questions." But that wasn't it at all.

When we asked Brad later on why he ultimately partnered with SoulPancake, he said in his usual low-key drawl: "I figured if you had a guy from Tennessee on your team, you must be okay."

We never thought that the Kid President journey would take us where it has—from a locker room Pep Talk to the White House to Beyoncé's arms. But it did. And along the way, this sweet, charismatic child and his genius big brother have made a movement out of solving homelessness, inspiring teachers to change the way classrooms operate, and helping contribute to ending childhood hunger. Along the way, they celebrate hope, love, dancing, and corndogs.

When I agreed to write the preface to this book, I wasn't sure what more there was to say about Brad and Robby and their magnificent brainchild. But as I thought more about it, I realized there are three qualities that came together in a perfect storm to create the Kid President phenomenon. The one I've already mentioned is joy. Joy in tone and execution. And in the hearts and smiles of millions of viewers. The second is an obvious one—talent. Brad and Robby are brilliant together. Period.

But the final factor that I think is often forgotten in what makes Kid President magical is the power of encouragement.

Most people who have heard the Kid President story are familiar with the fact that Robby Novak suffers from a brittle bone condition that has caused him pain, countless broken bones, and more hospital visits than any child should ever have. But you'd never know that by looking at his infectious grin. The reason for this is his parents: They have never once told him that he can't do something because his bones might break. And that has made all the difference.

Meanwhile, Brad Montague was raised on a farm in a town with a smaller population than my local Costco. Growing up, the Muppets were his friends and writing stories was a pastime. Despite this, creativity wasn't something "real"—it was just for fun, a hobby. But one day, his 4th-grade teacher told him: You matter. You have a voice. You are important. Suddenly, Brad felt someone really believed in him. So he started to create. And create. And create. And the rest is history.

I am grateful that Robby's parents and Brad's teacher were free with their loving words. It was the results of that encouragement (paired with talent and joy) that led to the Kid President revolution.

It also reminds me that when you have a choice of what to say, choosing kindness and encouragement can change the course of the future. It's my sincere hope that SoulPancake has been able to do justice to the mission of Kid President and will continue to be a creator and encourager of inspiring, joyful content that changes the world.

But most of all, I want to thank Robby, Brad, and their legions of fans for helping us throw the greatest dance party of all time.

— RAINN

MEET BRAD & ROBBY

BRAD MONTAGUE
DIRECTOR

Brad Montague is a 33-year-old guy from Tennessee and Robby's brother-in-law. He created Kid President. He likes to make stuff and believes in encouraging cooperation between kids and grown-ups. Brad loves cartoons, the films of Jacques Tati, eggrolls, and fart noises.

Robby Novak, aka Kid President, is an 11-year-old boy from Tennessee. He loves dancing, playing the drums, spending time with friends, video games, making the world more awesome, and fart noises.

Robby Novak has always inspired me. Many people around the world know him as Kid President, but to me he's Robby. He's family.

It's funny to see people react when he introduces me as his brother-in-law. I am, after all, 20 years older than him and several shades lighter. Yet somehow he doesn't seem to care about those differences or even see them. He just sees me. To him I'm Brad. I'm family.

Kids are awesome like that. They see things differently. Where I might see a handrail to go down stairs, he sees a slide. Where I might see a puddle of water, he sees a perfect place to jump. Where I might be quick to see the differences between myself and someone else, he's quick to make a friend. That's what happens when you look for the best in the world.

Robby and I first met when he was just a few months old, and every day since, he's taught me how to look at everything with fresh eyes. In doing so he's shown me what it means to live with wonder, courage, joy, and strength. Together, the two of us have been on a wild adventure—the kind we never dreamed we could—but that's how all the best adventures go.

"Let's make a video."

We come from a creative family. Robby and I have always made things together: songs, drawings, home movies. So when my wife and I got the idea to dress him up in a suit and ask him his thoughts on politics, it wasn't a strange request. My mother-in-law ordered a small black suit. She looked for the cheapest she could find, never imagining it would be the same suit her son would wear to meet the real president of the United States just a few short months later. (We still use cheap suits, by the way. Robby likes to roll around on the ground.)

We live just a few houses down from each other in a small Tennessee town. It was a warm summer afternoon when he and his mom walked over to our house to film the first video. Decked out in his fancy new suit, Robby announced himself as he entered. He pretty much always makes a big entrance just to make me laugh—singing, "I'm here!" or occasionally ringing the doorbell and then hiding so he can pop out and surprise me. Though those are bold entrances, on this particular day he was even bolder as he bounded through the doorway. Not having had much experience in formal wear, he enjoyed the novelty of adjusting his tie, throwing his jacket on and off, and saying the word "swag" a lot.

Left
Brad plays with 2-year-old Robby on the beach.

Center
Robby, age 6, playing in the backyard.

Right
Brad and 3-year-old Robby at Disney World in 2006.

Would anyone hear a happy, small voice over the louder, older ones?

This was the summer of 2012, and our country was in the middle of a heated presidential race. As they do during any election, people were passionately debating each side. It seemed like everyone had a strong opinion. You couldn't go anywhere online without seeing someone post something about the election (often aggressive and frequently misspelled).

Kid President grew out of a desire to put something online that would diffuse the whole political conversation and simply be funny. I didn't think the world needed a kid as president of the United States. I just thought the world needed grown-ups to pause and see things through the eyes of a kid. *What if a kid just told everybody what they thought? What if that kid was Robby? Would anyone hear a happy, small voice over the louder, older ones?*

As it turns out, yes.

I hit record, and what happened next would be the start of an unexpected journey that would take us all over the world.

My wife, Robby's sister Kristi, helped turn one of the rooms in our house into a little studio. We drew a presidential seal on a large sheet of cardboard, which my wife then colored in. The desk we used was an old record player I had discovered earlier that year on the side of the road. Using duct tape, I placed two small American flags on either side of the desk. The finishing touch was a name card at the edge of the desk scribbled with his title: PRESIDENT (because who could argue with that?).

We didn't discuss much before filming. I simply said, "You're the president. This is your chance to tell all the grown-ups of the world what you want them to hear."

Before I could give any more direction, he stepped behind the desk and immediately started dancing. A lot. So much dancing, in fact, that I finally had to ask him to stop so we could make a video that wasn't just dancing. He paused for a moment, looked at me, and then immediately started dancing again. We both collapsed with laughter.

I hit record, and what happened next would be the start of an unexpected journey that would take us all over the world—from the White House, to creating a television show, and even to writing this very book you are reading. (Thanks, by the way.) Like all the ones that would follow it, our first shoot was filled with dancing and laughing and then more dancing.

Opposite
Brad and Robby after shooting the very first Kid President video ever, in July 2012.

Above Left
Robby and Brad do the first can phone interview in August 2012. The guest on the other line is the *Adventure Time* creator, Pen Ward!

Above Right
Robby being Robby, even when the camera isn't rolling.

I posted the first video thinking it would be the only one. Family and friends enjoyed it, so we made another. As more and more people watched, it became clear this strange little platform we had created could be used to point people toward things that we felt really mattered. Yes, the videos were silly, but at the heart of each one was a message. I had discovered a fun way for the two of us to spend time together and, at the same time, share things we cared about with the world.

I had discovered a fun way for the two of us to spend time together and, at the same time, share things we cared about with the world.

We created videos urging people to put down their phones and talk to the people around them, to stop complaining and start celebrating, to hug more and shout less. I hoped they would be entertaining, but the main purpose was to create something inspiring and contagious enough that people actually lived them out. I made it my mission to let all the videos be a joyful vision of how the world could be. In the process, I learned a lot about what was important to me. I discovered these weren't just things I wanted the world to know, but things I wanted Robby to know.

Early on we received several emails asking Kid President what political party he supported. I found this funny since Kid President is a fictional character but thought it'd be interesting to see what Robby thought. Before every shoot, I usually lay out the topic we're going to cover and discuss it with him a bit beforehand. I began explaining to him the political party system. I shared with him the philosophies behind the Republican and Democratic parties. Just as I was going into what it meant to be a Libertarian, he interrupted me and said, "I'm not in a party! I am a party!"

"Yep," I thought. "That's much better than what I was going to say."

He's always teaching me.

"There's always a reason to dance."

Many people have no idea that Robby was born with a bone condition called osteogenesis imperfecta. Often referred to as "brittle bone disease," this genetic condition causes a person's bones to break easily—many times for little or no reason at all. Because of his condition, Robby has now had more than 70 broken bones and 13 orthopedic surgeries, yet you'd have to look hard to see any hint of pain in the silly web videos we create together.

Many doctors said he would likely never walk, and I guess they were right. He dances. He's a picture of what it means to rebel joyfully against your circumstances.

Opposite
Backstage on the set of the Kid President television show, *Kid President: Declaration of Awesome.*

Top Right
Brad assists 5-year-old Robby at a Special Needs Athletics game in April 2009.

Center Right
4-year-old Robby still having fun despite having both legs casted after surgery.

Bottom Right
Brad visiting 2-year-old Robby in the hospital during his first rodding surgery in November 2005.

I remember one particularly rough patch when Robby was just 4 years old. Two back-to-back surgeries for femur re-rodding resulted in him being confined to bed in a bright-red full-body cast. Going to visit him I was prepared to be tough. I had never seen him this broken and did not want to cry in front of him. Of course, he was the tough one. I walked in to see him lying on his little bed with a huge smile on his face, listening to music, and using the only body parts he could move (his toes, fingers, and head) to dance.

It's this resilient spirit that I think comes through in our most viewed video, *A Pep Talk from Kid President to You.* The more than 33 million people seeing him and hearing the words he spoke had no clue that the child speaking them knew a thing or two about needing a pep talk. They simply heard something we all need to hear sometimes: "You were made to be awesome. Keep going." I think it connected with people because it's true.

"You were made to be awesome. Keep going."

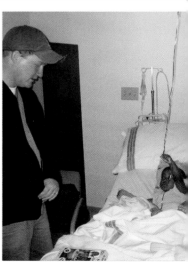

Kid President represents a joyful rebellion. Typically, rebellions are fueled by anger. They result in shouting and fights and tea being thrown into large bodies of water. But I think the best movements are fueled by a joyful vision of what could be. There's the way things are in the world, and there's the way things could be. We want to help make things as they should be. We want to make things, as Kid President would say, "more awesome."

A joyful rebellion is you living differently not because you're mad at how things are but because you are swelling with joy at the thought of how things could be. When you joyfully rebel against your circumstances, against mediocrity or negativity, you invite others into something really beautiful.

Robby's perseverance and outlook on life have invited me into something beautiful. They've made me want to be a little rebel for joy. They've made it hard for me ever to complain about any small problem or headache I might have. They've made me want to make the world more awesome.

I mean, if he can find a reason to dance, maybe we can, too.

Your friend,

BRAD

A joyful rebellion is you living differently not because you're mad at how things are, but because you are swelling with joy at the thought of how things could be.

Above

This photo is from the SoulPancake-inspired ballpit at Catalyst West in Irvine, CA.

About *this* Book

Hello, and welcome to our book.

BRAD — What do you think about that for the first line?

No way, man! — ROBBY

Too formal. How about . . .

It's you! We're so excited you picked up our book.
We've been waiting for you.

That. Is. Creepy.

Ugh. Yep. Sorry. Let me try again. . . .

If you're reading this very first sentence in our book,
we need you to know that the future of human existence
is in your hands.

Um . . . No.

Too much. Here, let's try this:

This is the first sentence in our book.

What do you think?

Perfect.

How to Use This Book

You've already opened it, so that's a good start.
Next, you should read it.
Then you should go be awesome. Deal? Thanks.

It's a pretty bold move to make our first book a GUIDE TO BEING AWESOME. It sort of implies we somehow think we've got it all figured out. Do you have it all figured out?

No. I've never written a book before.

Well, I'll help you with that. I'm learning, too.

We're learning to write a book. We're learning to be awesome. We're learning lots of things!

So, you think it's okay if we reveal to the readers of this book that we don't have being awesome all figured out?

Um . . . do we have to?

We don't have to . . . but if we want to be honest, then I think we should. Do you want the book to be honest?

That's a loaded question, man.

(Laughs)

Okay. Let's be honest: I am not always awesome. Brad is not always awesome. The people reading this are not always awesome.

Whoa! Easy now. You just unloaded a lot on these people.

Apologies, people.

Yes, the title of this book is *Kid President's Guide to Being Awesome*, but we readily admit to you, our new friends, that we don't have being awesome all figured out. We do know awesome when we see it, though. And there seems to be a common formula:

Do you want to be awesome? Treat people awesome.

This book is our attempt to share a few ways we've seen awesome spread. We hope that by sharing these thoughts, you and your loved ones will be encouraged to do good. You'll see stories of people who have inspired us. Some of these people are young, and some are not so young. Some of these people are well-known, and some are not. But they are all awesome; they are all guided by a sense that things can be better.

You don't have to commit to doing everything we mention in here. We would love, though, if you'd take at least a few and make them happen. There's even some space at the end where you can add ideas of your own. (Awesome is always a work in progress!) We're confident you're gonna make something wonderful happen, and we're happy you've joined us on our next great adventure.

It is our hope that you are inspired as you go through this book to do something of your own to make the world more awesome. People like you are what have kept us encouraged and going. We can't wait to see what you help make happen next. And if you decide to go out and make something happen, please share it with us: www.kidpresident.com/book.

Do you want to be awesome? Treat people awesome.

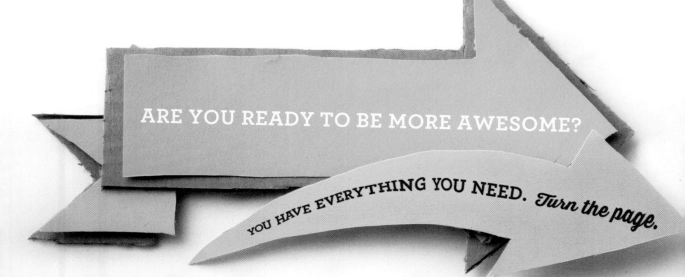

ARE YOU READY TO BE MORE AWESOME?

YOU HAVE EVERYTHING YOU NEED. *Turn the page.*

ABOUT the WORD

AWE

awe·some

ˈô-səm

adjective

Definition: A word that was once reserved strictly for moments, ideas, and experiences that caused someone to feel awe, now "awesome" is used to describe anything from the Grand Canyon to carpet cleaner. Kid President uses the word "awesome" because the world really does fill him with awe. Sure there are other adjectives, but they're used for things that aren't awesome.

A BRIEF HISTORY OF "AWESOME"

1598

The word "awesome" appears for the first time in the Oxford English Dictionary.

1701

Composer Johann Sebastian Bach performs one of his first pieces of music. His next-door neighbor hears and deems it "awesome."

1776

After Thomas Jefferson checks rough draft of Declaration of Independence for spelling and grammar, the document is declared "awesome."

1879

Thomas Edison says the word "awesome" after a little lightbulb goes off in his head, and he files a patent for the "lightbulb."

SOME

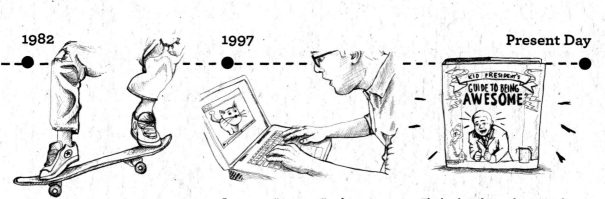

1982

A young skateboarder says "awesome" as he reacts to his fellow skateboarder's sick ollie.

1997

A guy says "awesome" as he watches the first cat video posted online. He attempts to print it out and share with his friends at work.

Present Day

The book *Kid President's Guide to Being Awesome* is released and breaks all sorts of awesome records because it is so awesome.

I think we all need a pep talk.

The world needs you to stop being boring. Yeah, you. Boring is easy.
Everybody can be boring. But you're gooder than that.

Life is not a game, people. Life isn't a cereal, either. (Well, it is a cereal.)
And if life is a game, are we on the same team? I mean really, right?
I'm on your team; be on my team.

This is life, people. You got air coming through your nose; you got a heartbeat.
That means it's time to do something.

A poem: *Two roads diverged in the woods, and I took the road less traveled . . .* and it hurt, man! Really bad! Rocks, thorns, and glass . . . My pants broke! Why?

Not cool, Robert Frost.

But what if there really were two paths?
I would want to be on the one that leads to awesome.

Just like that dude Journey said, "Don't stop believing . . . unless your dream is stupid, then you should get a better dream." I think that's how it goes.

Get a better dream, then keep going, keep going, keep going, keep going.

What if Michael Jordan had quit? (Well, he did quit. No, he retired. Yeah, that's right; he retired.) But before that, in high school, what if he quit when he didn't make the team? He would've never made *Space Jam*. And I love *Space Jam*.

What will be your *Space Jam*? What will you create that will make the world awesome? Nothing, if you keep sitting there. That's why I'm talking to you today. This is your time. This is my time. This is our time.

We can make every day better for each other. But if we're all on the same team, let's start acting like it. We got work to do. We can cry about it or we can dance about it. We were made to be awesome. Let's get out there!

I don't know everything; I'm just a kid. But I do know this: It's everybody's duty to give the world a reason to dance. So get to it!

You've just been pep talked.
Create something that will make the world awesome. Play ball.

ABOUT THE PEP TALK

It was a cold Tennessee January when we filmed "A Pep Talk from Kid President to You." The election was over, and we thought our work would be winding down. We had just experienced the accidental success of creating a few simple web videos that had caught on with people. In the process of doing something we loved, we had built a nice little community of people online. Because of this we got to team up with the good people at SoulPancake. We had the pleasure of doing videos with cool people like Andrew W.K. and Josh Groban and Dave Coulier. This was already more than we ever imagined we'd get to do. We were happy and honored.

In our minds, this pep talk was a way to close this chapter and return to our normal lives. We wanted to make it special because we thought: This might be one of our final opportunities to say what we want to say as Kid President.

As it turns out, it was just the beginning.

The response was immediate. Within just a handful of days, our little video found its way across the desks and news feeds of more than 3 million people. As of this writing it has been viewed more than 34 million times. We found out that millions of people around the globe thought that the world needed a pep talk, too.

As of this writing it has been viewed more than 34 million times.

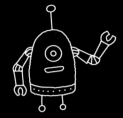

The video has been parodied. (One of our favorites was a "Kid Rabbi" giving a pep talk.) Lines from it have popped up on T-shirts, posters, bumper stickers, and all throughout various media. ("Not cool, Robert Frost!" has been spotted many times on school bulletin boards and unauthorized products like drink koozies.) The video has been Auto-Tuned, remixed, and debated. (Several bloggers wrote lengthy think pieces on what the message and virality of our video meant.) How did this happen?

As the view counts rose, email and phone calls poured in. We were completely overwhelmed and had to call an emergency family meeting. There were major questions that needed answering: Which morning show will you go on? Can Kid President be in our horror movie? Do you have an agent? and on and on and on. We had to pause, take a deep breath, and collectively answer the actual important question: What story do we, as a family, want to tell?

It's a conversation we should have had long before having a video go viral on the internet. It's a question we should have been asking all along. It's what has helped guide our every decision since, and it's even what helped us as we thought about what we wanted to say with this book.

Opposite
Shooting one of the last scenes for the Pep Talk video, just a few days before the video was posted online.

Where do you want to go? What story do you want to tell? We hope this book helps you and all the people around you to think and get moving. With every decision you make, you're saying something. We want to say something awesome, and we want you to say something awesome, too.

"What will you create that will make the world more awesome?"

CHAPTER 1:

Life

is what happens when you
★ PUT DOWN ★
YOUR PHONE

#1
PUT
DOWN
YOUR
PHONE

We're always surprised at what connects most with people who watch one of our videos. In the video "Kid President's Open Letter to Moms," we included a brief line about putting down your phone. It was a simple joke about how you should put down your phone, unless someone in your family is named Phone. (The next piece of advice was to not name your kid Phone.)

We had no clue that millions of people would watch and share that video. We also had no clue that more than half of the people watching the video would see it on their mobile devices. That probably helped it touch a nerve. Just days after the video was posted, we received email after email from people telling us how it inspired them to have a phone-free weekend. One mother emailed us to tell us she was inspired to totally get rid of her phone. (We thought this was a bit extreme, but hey, whatever it takes.)

It does, however, tap into something we're all trying to figure out: How can we really be present? Technology is amazing. We humans are more connected than ever, but sometimes it can disconnect us from all the people we love most. One big step to being awesome is remembering to treat the people right in front of you awesome.

Maybe there's something getting in the way for you.

Lots of [our] really
cool moments...
aren't documented
with a photo.
It kind of
made us happy.
It's somehow
actually cooler
that we got
to fully be
part of
those moments
together.

Above
Robby couldn't stop laughing about the strange names moms sometimes give their kids when we made our "Open Letter to Moms" video.

And it's not just phones. There were times when our family was so busy taking photos and filming our adventures that we forgot to actually enjoy them. We had to rethink all the stuff that was getting in the way of us really enjoying and experiencing our time together. In creating this book, we realized there are lots of really cool moments that happened along our journey that aren't documented with a photo. It kind of made us happy. It's somehow actually cooler that we got to fully be part of those moments together. It's like they only exist in what Robby calls "brain pictures."

#2 TAKE BRAIN PICTURES

So, what exactly are brain pictures?

They are pictures you take with your brain.

I know that. You know what I'm asking! Tell me more.

It's times in your life that you want to capture and remember forever.

Nice. Like what?

Going somewhere new and cool. Having a really good day. Seeing a cloud in the sky that looks like something and you really want to remember it.

I like that. What are some clouds that you've really wanted to remember?

I forgot.

There are lots of times you just have to remember to take brain pictures. These are the moments you absolutely need to experience life, not through a camera or a screen, but directly through your eyeballs. Taking these brain pictures will help you later on in your journey. You'll be happy you took them. Make a note of the moments in your life when you want to be fully present.

Here are a few of Kid President's brain picture moments.

Enjoying a perfectly crisp corndog.

Hitting that perfect dance move at just the right point in your favorite song.

The moment when you think there's only one piece of Bubble Wrap left to pop, but you learn there's an entire row left.

Walking into the United Nations General Assembly Hall for the first time.

Realizing your mustache is finally coming in.

Your mustache is not coming in.

Look closer, man.

Nope, still don't see it.

You need to get your eyes checked.*

Don't focus on presents. FOCUS ON BEING PRESENT.

Relax.

don't sweat the small stuff.
life is short and deodorant is expensive.

#4 Be Less **Busy** and

BE More **Awesome**

It's easy to get busy. We have important places to be, things to do, an entire world to make more awesome. It can get overwhelming. It's time to take a look at your to-do list and make sure you're busy with the right stuff. It's time to make time for what life is really about.

You get 86,400 seconds in a day to make the world more awesome. There are 365 days in a year, so that works out to 8,760 hours (or 8,784 if it happens to be a leap year). This means you have more than 31.5 million seconds each year to make the world more awesome. You can't be too busy for awesome. Make every second count.

Above

Kid President made this gum ball machine using an upside-down planter, a fishbowl, and the lid from his mom's cookie jar (sorry, Mom).

Kid President created this gum ball machine to help him remember to make every day awesome. It has been filled with 365 gum balls, representing the number of days in a year. Each tasty gum ball is a reminder that you could spend each day however you want. You could quickly chew each one up, then spit it out without really enjoying it, or you could take the time to savor and really appreciate each one. Either way, you only get so many. They are your days. Make them awesome.

Celebrate today. EVERY BREATH IS A BIG DEAL.

LET'S LIVE IN A WORLD WITH MORE HIGH FIVES

The Traditional

A celebratory meeting between two friends—or soon-to-be friends—where palms connect as arms are raised about head-high.

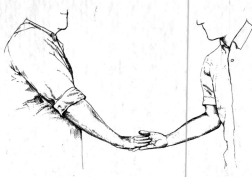

The Low Five

A variation on the Traditional high five in which the participants lower their hands and connect with palms horizontal.

The Fist Bump

While technically not a high five, this is a gesture of camaraderie and friendship having several variations of its own (example, the exploding fist bump, which features sound effects, or the cradled fist bump, where the hand goes over the fist).

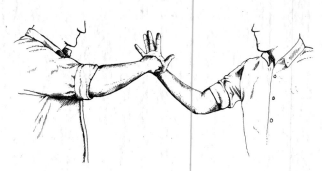

The Turkey

A hybrid where the Fist Bump meets the Traditional high five to create the illusion of a turkey.

Why high fives?

It lets people know you're friends.

That's a good point. You do hand out lots of high fives.

Yes. To everybody. Except to people who are scared of them.

There are people who are scared of high fives?

Well, yeah. If they've never seen one before, they might think you're going to hit them.

Good point.

The Long Jump
This option for thrill-seeking high fivers is a great way to display athletic skill while also letting your friend—or soon-to-be friend—know you care.

The Virtual High Five
This is a way to celebrate friendship via phone or email when far from each other or in person when both parties happen to be in the same room but do not want to get up.

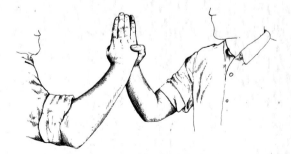

The Hand Hug
A variation on the Traditional high five where the thumbs wrap around to create two hands hugging.

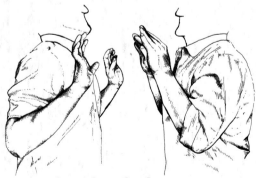

The Awkward Velociraptor
Both parties pretend to be dinosaurs who have very small arms and cannot quite reach the other person's hand.

#6
BRING
AWESOME
BACK

What JUSTIN TIMBERLAKE
taught us about pocket squares
and being awesome

We are often asked what it's like to meet famous people. Are they nice in real life? Are they as tall as you thought they would be? Did you wash your hands after shaking theirs? While the answers to that vary, one thing we've certainly learned is that famous people are just that: people.

It was an awesome day when we found out that one of the fans of our videos was none other than Justin Timberlake. THE Justin Timberlake. Pop superstar, actor, fellow suit-and-tie enthusiast. We got extremely excited and our imaginations ran wild. Would we get to meet him? Would he be super cool in real life? Could we become best friends, wear matching slap bracelets, and start our own band?

We did get to meet Justin and it was awesome, though for reasons we didn't anticipate. We were invited to one of his shows and we freaked out. There, we got to join him backstage where we ate pizza, met his wife, Jessica Biel, talked about basketball—the Memphis Grizzlies—and learned how to fold pocket squares. Instead of acting like he was the famous one, we were treated like royalty. He did everything he could to put

pocKet square!

us both at ease as he listened, laughed, and made us feel like we should offer him up our autographs. He wanted to hear all about Robby's school and family and pets. It was as if we were the famous ones—that is until his grandmother entered the room.

He stood and introduced us to his grandmother. She hugged him and us. She then proceeded to tell him how much she enjoyed the show. It was clear his grandmother had been following along on the tour. We watched as they talked and, in that moment, learned something very important: Nobody is more important than your grandmother.

Nobody is more important than your grandmother.

We learned a lot from Justin Timberlake that night. Sure we learned how to fold pocket squares, and that was pretty cool, but the coolest thing we learned was how to treat people like they matter. What if we treated all grandmothers like they were famous? What if we treated everybody like they deserved all of our attention?

Celebrities are called "celebrities" because society has somehow decided they are people worth celebrating. Let's create a society where we celebrate everybody. Let's live in a world where little brothers, 4th-grade teachers, firefighters, and grandmas are treated like they just performed for an entire arena.

Maybe our goal as people shouldn't be to become a celebrity, but to live in a way that makes everyone around us feel celebrated.

#7

If it doesn't make the world better, don't do it

We all have barriers keeping us from being as awesome as we can be. Maybe this simple little rule could help us question our actions and, if needed, refrain from the ones that don't make the world better.

Much of this book has things we should all add to our to-do lists, but here are a few to add to our "not-do" list:

- ☐ Don't stop believing . . . unless your dream is stupid. (See page 31.)
- ☐ Don't type in all caps.
- ☐ Don't be a bully. (Don't even be a bully to the bullies. That just makes more bullies.)
- ☐ Don't be mean. Be meaningful.
- ☐ Don't keep score.

What would you add to your not-do list?

A NOTE FROM BRAD

It sounds simple, and maybe it is. Years before we started Kid President, I was having a conversation with Robby about what people should do to make the world a better place. His response was, "If it doesn't make the world better, people just shouldn't do it." I smiled, but as we grown-ups tend to do, I immediately dismissed it. "Sure this is a sweet idea," I thought, "but isn't it just oversimplifying the many complicated issues we face in the world today?"

The idea stuck with me, though. "If it doesn't make the world better, don't do it." I found myself thinking about it and applying it to how I did everything. I thought about it in how I spent my money. Does buying this make the world better? I thought about it when dealing with people. Does sending this angry email make the world better?

I realized that, yes, the world is full of many complicated, nuanced issues, but I really think things would look a lot different if we could all approach life with this simple question: Does this make the world better?

YOUR FRIEND,
Brad

CHAPTER 2:
FOCUS
ON THE AWESOME

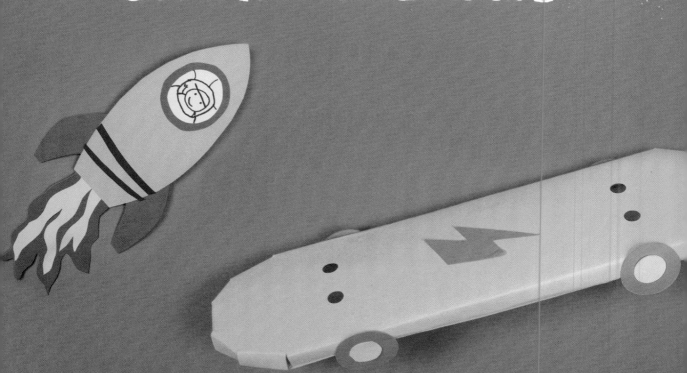

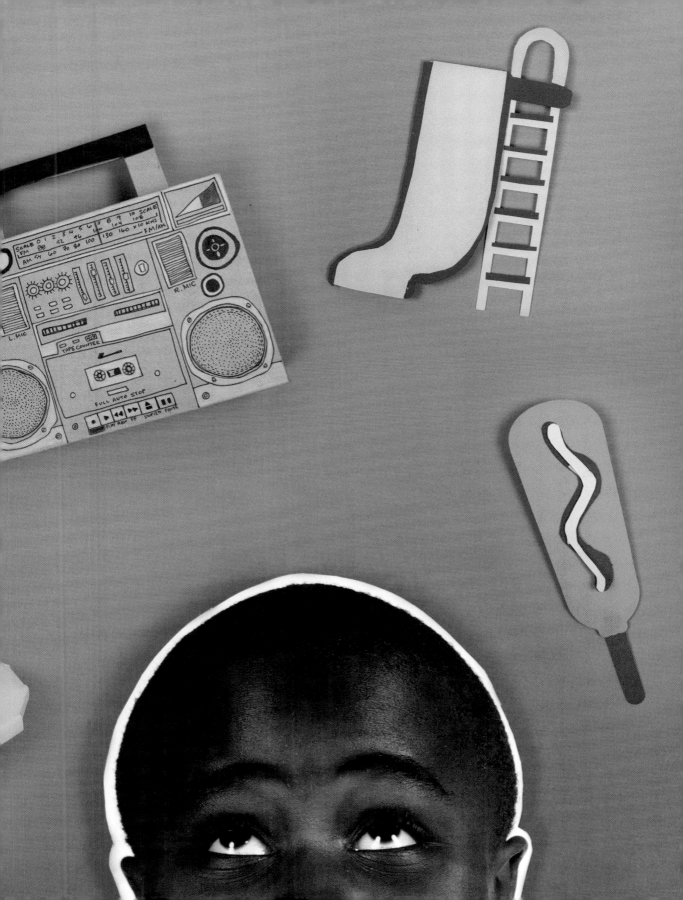

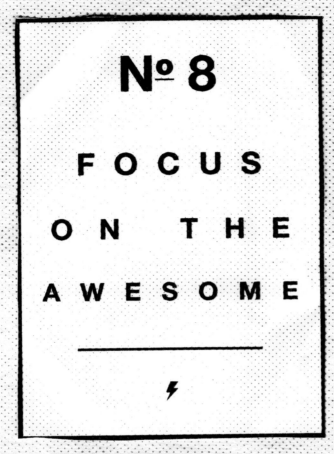

You'll come across plenty of things along your journey that aren't awesome. Some days it will seem like there's more bad than good, but you know that's not true. On days when it's hard to see the awesome, keep looking. It's there.

AWESOME-TINTED GLASSES!
Now available!

So how do you focus on the awesome on days when it's hard to see?

Like what do you mean?

Well, you've had bad days before, right?

Yeah. Plenty of them.

How do you stay positive when things are tough?

When things are tough, you just have to look for the awesome. Like when you are in the hospital just think about the hamburgers.

Hamburgers? You've lost me here.

The hospital I go to has really good hamburgers.

That's what keeps you going?

Yeah.

The hamburgers in the hospital are that good?

They're good enough for me to talk about them right now, aren't they?

Point taken.

How to look at the world through awesome-tinted glasses:

Remember to look for it.

———

Invent special glasses that help you only see things that are awesome.

———

Surround yourself with people who help you see it.

Your day won't always be filled with awesome. Your day might be filled with traffic, bad grades, a broken bone, or even worse. Keep your focus on the awesome. It's not always easy to see, but it's always there. Create a list of things that keep you going. Keep it nearby. You'll be glad you did.

HOW TO SEE THE AWESOME AROUND YOU: *An Example*

We all see things differently. If you'd like proof, here is a real-life example. On the left is Brad's experience of traveling to New York for a movie premiere (it's a postcard to his wife). On the right is an essay Robby wrote for school about the same experience.

NEW YORK CITY

KRISTI!!!

TODAY I MET EMMA STONE.

YES. YOU READ THAT RIGHT.

EMMA STONE!

JUST HAD TO LET YOU KNOW I MET EMMA (THAT'S WHAT I CALL HER BECAUSE WE'RE FRIENDS NOW)

WHAT IS LIFE?!?

love,
    BRAD

P.S. EMMA STONE!

KRISTI MONTAGUE
P.O. BOX 41791
MEMPHIS, TN 38174

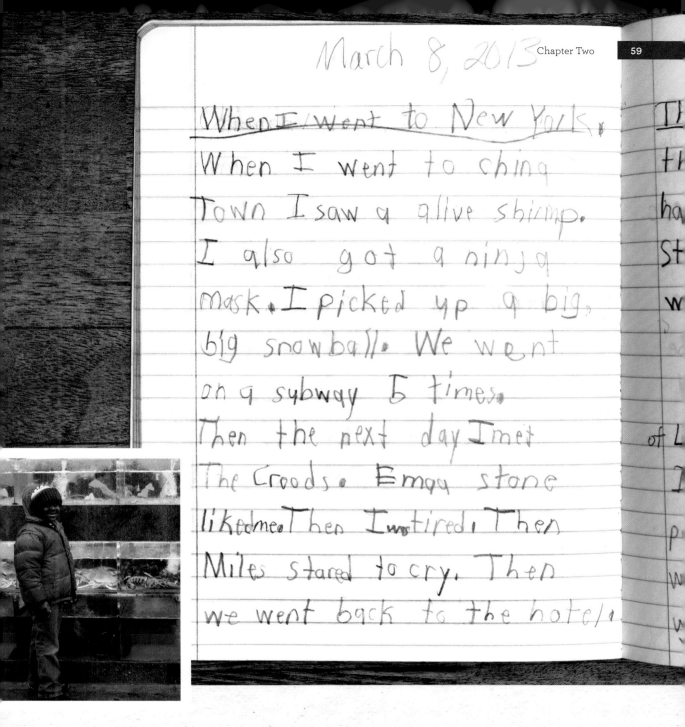

March 8, 2013

When I went to New York.
When I went to china
Town I saw a alive shrimp.
I also got a ninja
mask. I picked up a big,
big snowball. We went
on a subway 5 times.
Then the next day I met
The Croods. Emma stone
liked me. Then I was tired. Then
Miles started to cry. Then
we went back to the hotel.

Sometimes we need other people to
help us remember to look for and see
the awesome. It's there. Keep looking.

#9 Look :FOR: WHAT MATTERS

Since he was 14, **YASH GUPTA** has been collecting eyeglasses for those in need. Now, he helps run an organization called Sight Learning. We spoke to Yash about his project.

It seems like your life changed when you broke your glasses. Can you tell us what happened?
I broke my glasses my freshman year of high school sparring in taekwondo. I had been wearing glasses since I was only 5 years old, so I had begun taking them for granted. I really began to appreciate glasses when I was forced to go to school without them as a new pair was made. As I sat in the back of class, I ultimately realized how essential glasses were to my ability to learn. After doing research, I learned that millions of students lack the very eyeglasses that we discard by the millions here in North America.

What advice would you give to people who want to help solve a problem, but don't know how to start?
My advice is to start somewhere. Start out small, and you never know how big your small little project may end up becoming. Every person doing a little to solve a problem adds up to a lot of good being done for the world.

What's your favorite part of giving a kid a new pair of glasses?
One of my favorite parts of Sight Learning is organizing and going on eye clinic trips to developing nations we donate glasses to. At these eye clinics, we work with optometrists and volunteers to give free eye care to students and their families who cannot afford them. The emotion the children and their families feel when putting on a pair of glasses for the first time is indescribable. Initially, the children are confused, because they aren't used to seeing the world as clearly as they finally are. Then slowly, they'll start realizing that this is how it's meant to be and an overwhelming sense of joy creeps onto their faces.

What's next for Sight Learning?
Sight Learning has collected and distributed more than $1 million worth of used eyeglasses, equivalent to more than 20,000 pairs. We now have chapters in 14 different U.S. states and 4 different countries helping us collect used eyeglasses, and we look forward to increasing these numbers in the future.

What's the best way for people to help with Sight Learning?
The best way to help Sight Learning is to donate glasses to us by mailing them to us at 1 League #60715, Irvine, CA 92602

What keeps you going?
For me, what keeps me going is seeing the joy on those children's faces as they run around with their new pair of glasses. Realizing that something that is being wasted can be put to use and change another person's life is an incredible feeling and makes me want to do more and more.

YASH GUPTA
California, USA

Why He's Awesome:
- He works to distribute glasses to those in need.
- His organization, Sight Learning, has distributed more than 20,000 pairs of used eyeglasses.
- His name rhymes with "dash."

#10
AS HUMAN
BEINGS,
WE ARE
CAPABLE OF
LOTS OF
BAD STUFF,
BUT ALSO
CUPCAKES.

#11

COMPLAIN LESS.
Celebrate more.

There's always something to complain about. With social media, there are now more places to complain about things than ever before, but you're not interested in that. You're looking for reasons to celebrate

#12 GET OUT THERE!

When we found out that actress and philanthropist **OLIVIA WILDE** often travels to Haiti, a place our family has also visited, we were excited to talk to her about her passion for travel and other people.

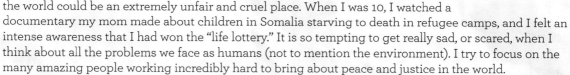

You are awesome! How did you get so awesome?
Why, thank you! I believe true awesomeness comes from experience, and so I like to think I get awesomer with every challenge I face and every lesson I learn. I try to live with my eyes, ears, and heart open to newness, even if it's initially kind of scary. People change constantly; it's important to remember we are never finished products.

When did you realize the world was big and full of problems and how did you keep from getting sad and giving up completely? Apologies for the big sentence there. I just really need to know!
Well, my parents are both journalists working in some of the toughest places on Earth, so I knew from a really young age that the world could be an extremely unfair and cruel place. When I was 10, I watched a documentary my mom made about children in Somalia starving to death in refugee camps, and I felt an intense awareness that I had won the "life lottery." It is so tempting to get really sad, or scared, when I think about all the problems we face as humans (not to mention the environment). I try to focus on the many amazing people working incredibly hard to bring about peace and justice in the world.

What made you want to do work in Haiti?
I went to Haiti as a small child with my family, and it stuck in my mind as a magical place. I was desperate to return one day. As soon as I could, I went back as an adult and found the same beautiful country I remembered, suffering from crippling poverty. I began working with an organization called Artists for Peace and Justice, which supports a local group in Port-au-Prince, working to bring education, health care, and basic infrastructure to the community. Then the earthquake hit in 2010, and our operation went into overdrive. I began to travel down to Haiti frequently, falling more in love with the country and its people with every visit.

Things can get pretty tough. What keeps you going?
Stories of people overcoming unimaginable odds and exercising their power as human beings to make the world a better place.

How can kids and grown-ups reading this work together to make the world more awesome?
Do some soul-searching, and find out what inspires you, and then become actively involved in that, and make it your purpose. There are so many resources to find organizations working on projects of every imaginable type. Whether it's working in the oceans, forests, schools, refugee camps, hospitals, shelters, or zoos, there is a way you can be extremely helpful!

What are some things you love?
Tiny horses, giant dogs, spicy food, dance parties, '80s movies, waves, and hugs.

Finish this sentence: The world would be more awesome if _____.
Smurfs were real, chocolate was a vegetable, and we all realized how much we have in common.

#13 EVERY TIME YOU SEE A SLIDE, go down it

#14 Sing out loud.

You don't have
to have a reason to.

#15
LAUGH!

Help end global sadness.

#16 FOLLOW YOUR PASSION

What keeps you awake at night? What are your absolute favorite things in the world? What do you really care about? These are your passions.

> What are you passionate about?
>
> Basketball. Soccer. Dancing.
>
> All very active things.
>
> Yeah. I like to move.
>
> How does following your passion help make the world more awesome?
>
> Well, if you're doing something you love, then that means you're having fun and it will show.
>
> That's true. People will see and will want to be part of what you're doing.
>
> It's contagious, man.
>
> How can following your passions of basketball, soccer, and dancing help make the world more awesome?
>
> I'm still working on that.

It's not just things you love. You can also be passionate about solving a problem. We all have things in our lives that we'd really like to see be different. Anybody who has ever changed the world for the better asked themselves three questions. By answering these questions they got to the heart of what they are passionate about and how they could do something about it.

1. I'm not okay with _____.

2. I have _____.

3. I can _____.

Sometimes by following what you really love you can help solve a problem you really don't love. Take our friend **JACK ANDRAKA** for instance. He's passionate about science. (He loves it.) He's also passionate about finding a cure for cancer. (He doesn't love cancer.) By following his passion, he ended up doing something extraordinary.

1. I'M NOT OKAY WITH . . .

the 100 people who die of pancreatic cancer every day because no one has discovered a way to detect the disease before it becomes deadly. I hope to be part of a future where one day we can diagnose not just pancreatic cancer but all serious diseases with a simple, inexpensive, handheld device no larger than an iPhone while these diseases are in their earliest stages and can be treated. How amazing would that be?

2. I HAVE . . .

an interest in showing other youth how science is something you DO, not something you learn from a textbook. I want to show people that science isn't boring, like so many kids my age think, but SOOO much more exciting than taking selfie photos for Facebook or Instagram. Science is solving the mysteries of the universe. How could that be boring?!

3. I CAN . . .

help people by showing them that you don't need to have a fancy Ph.D. or even be old enough to drive a car to accomplish great things. All you need is the courage to ask the right questions, to believe in yourself, and to have a solid WiFi connection. If a kid who didn't even know what a pancreas was could discover an early detection method for pancreatic cancer, just imagine what you could do?

JACK ANDRAKA

Maryland, USA

Why He's Awesome:

- He invented an early detection test for pancreatic cancer when he was 15.
- He is the author of *Breakthrough: How One Teen Innovator Is Changing the World*.
- He met the First Lady, y'all!

CHAPTER 3:

Treat Everybody
LIKE IT'S THEIR
Birthday

#17 treat everybody like it's their BIRTHDAY

Birthdays are special. You might be thinking, "But if we treat everybody like it's their birthday every day, then the actual day of their birth won't be special." There are also additional concerns: overdoing it on cake, gift expenses, etc.

Hear us out, though.

everybody's worth celebrating. everybody matters.

Clockwise from Top Left
Fan art created by Artisa Tumiwa, an artist in Jakarta, Indonesia.

On the set of *Kid President: Declaration of Awesome*, just before filming a dance party.

Cupcakes!

Robby and Brad celebrate after the completion of filming the pilot episode of their TV show.

Treating everybody like it's their birthday isn't about constantly giving people gifts and birthday cake—though cake always helps. This is about remembering to celebrate people every single day. This rule applies not just to people who are your friends, but to everybody. It changes the way you see people, talk to people, and treat people.

Try it next time you're out anywhere. It can be the lady at the checkout line of the grocery store, the guy picking up trash, or the person walking their dog in the park. You don't have to yell "HAPPY BIRTHDAY!" or hand out balloons. Just give them your time and do whatever you can to let them know you think they're worth celebrating.

Everybody's worth celebrating. Everybody matters. Take time to let them know. Every day.

MAIL YOUR FRIEND A CORNDOG

In one of our early Kid President videos, we were trying to encourage people to do awesome things to surprise people. One of the suggestions in the video was "Mail your friend a corndog." The idea was that: 1) corndogs are tasty, and 2) people like surprises. We thought it'd be a nice gesture to surprise your friend with a corndog.

We didn't fully think through the whole corndog-in-the-mail idea. I guess we never thought people would actually do it, but they did. Days after the video went online, we began receiving messages from people who mailed corndogs to their friends. We also received photos of people holding up corndogs they had received in the mail.

As it turns out, mailing your friend a corndog isn't exactly the best idea. People do appreciate the fact that you thought of them, though. So that's still there. Time might take away the tastiness of the corndog, but it can't take away your thoughtfulness. That counts for something, right? Right?

So . . . you might be better off handing your corndog to your friend. They'll love the thought—and if you're lucky, they might even share.

Step 1
Get a corndog.

Step 2
Put the corndog
in a package.

Step 3
Mail the corndog to
your friend.

Step 4
Your friend is happy
because they just got
a corndog in the mail.

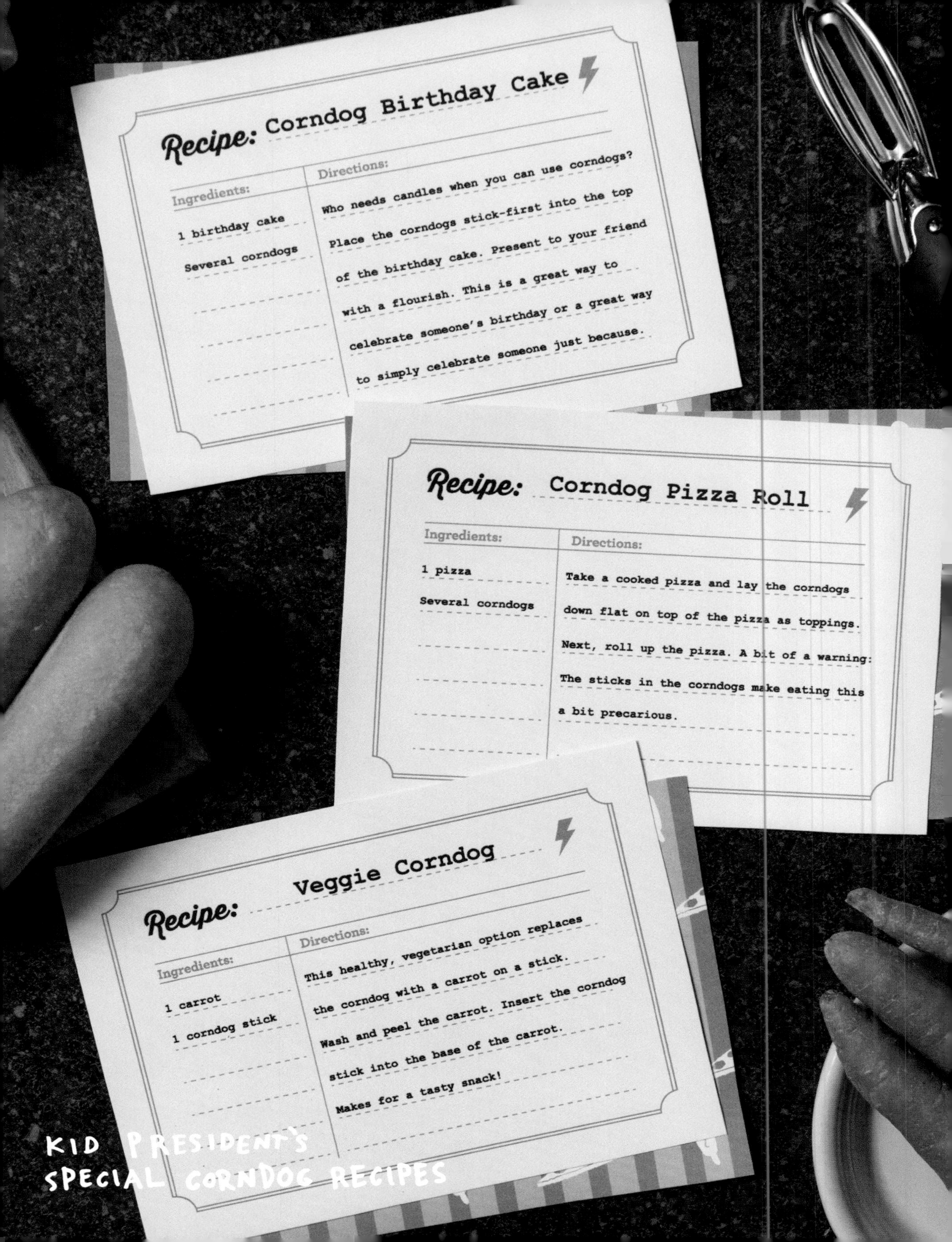

Recipe: Corndog Birthday Cake ⚡

Ingredients:

1 birthday cake

Several corndogs

Directions:

Who needs candles when you can use corndogs? Place the corndogs stick-first into the top of the birthday cake. Present to your friend with a flourish. This is a great way to celebrate someone's birthday or a great way to simply celebrate someone just because.

Recipe: Corndog Pizza Roll ⚡

Ingredients:

1 pizza

Several corndogs

Directions:

Take a cooked pizza and lay the corndogs down flat on top of the pizza as toppings. Next, roll up the pizza. A bit of a warning: The sticks in the corndogs make eating this a bit precarious.

Recipe: Veggie Corndog ⚡

Ingredients:

1 carrot

1 corndog stick

Directions:

This healthy, vegetarian option replaces the corndog with a carrot on a stick. Wash and peel the carrot. Insert the corndog stick into the base of the carrot. Makes for a tasty snack!

KID PRESIDENT'S
SPECIAL CORNDOG RECIPES

#19 HAVE A PIZZA DELIVERED TO SOMEONE YOU DISAGREE WITH

We first met our friend **BOB GOFF** a few years before starting our Kid President adventures and we're glad we did. Bob is a lawyer. He's a United States honorary consul to Uganda. He's founder of Restore International, an organization dedicated to helping kids in Uganda, India, Somalia, Iraq and Nepal. He's a bestselling author. Most of all, he's a great friend and teacher.

The last time we spoke you taught me a very valuable lesson about solving disagreements with pizza. Can you explain to my friends reading this book?
One of the things that comes with being a lawyer is you have people who are sore at you and you might be tempted to be sore at them. You sometimes run across people who disagree with you along the way. It really kind of takes away part of our humanity. I'm trying to have less enemies and so what I do is seek out people I haven't gotten along with for one reason or another and send them a pizza.

You just send them a pizza?
Yeah! Sometimes just sending a pizza is a beautiful way to say, "Man, I'm with ya." It's like breaking bread—except it's just flat and it's got cheese on it. There is just something wonderfully simple about that. Sometimes our love doesn't need to be super complex and you don't have to have all the words. Sometimes having whimsy will replace a whole lot of words. What's beautiful about that is that a lot of people fill in the words themselves. You know what I mean?

What about the disagreement? Does that really solve everything?
No. You aren't avoiding having a complicated discussion, but you are replacing that conflict with a real simple act of kindness and acceptance. You're just saying, "It's all good."

How did you grow up and keep your enthusiasm and joy?
You know what's very interesting—and I think it's true of many people—is that most of us are either a reflection of or reaction to the people who have been the closest to us. Wouldn't you agree?

Yeah . . .
Like, I'm a reflection of you and some of the beautiful things you guys are doing. And you might reflect some of the things that I'm doing. Everyone is trying to figure out if they are a victim. Forget about being a victim. Just be a beautiful reaction to everything.

You've done so much with your life. What's the secret to success?
I used to do all the stuff that I wanted to work, but now I want to do all the stuff that lasts. I've had about 100 great ideas that have worked, but I have had 20 stupid ideas that haven't worked. So working is not the standard anymore. I'm making decisions asking, "What is the shelf-life of this?" And being friends is always a safe bet. It has, like, infinite shelf-life.

BOB GOFF
California, USA

Why He's Awesome:
- He holds meetings at Disneyland on Tom Sawyer Island.
- He helps kids and grown-ups all over the world.
- He always answers his phone.

#20 EVERY ROOM YOU ENTER?

FREE HUGS!

Some people just need a hug. You know this. Hugs are a great way to let people know they can calm down. They don't have to work to impress you. You accept them just as they are. Hugs, though, can be tricky to navigate. To help you, we've created a simple chart of the variety of situations you might find yourself in. Use wisely.

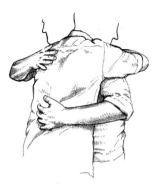

Classic Hug!
Tried and true, this hug really
is a classic.

Bro Hug!
Slightly less casual than the
Classic, the Bro Hug features a
light embrace followed by three
pats on the back.

Bear Hug!
Not to be confused with its much more
dangerous cousin Hugging a Real
Bear (which can lead to death), this
hug is big and typically reserved for
people you've met more than once.

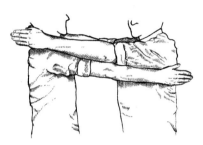

The Frankenstein!
A hug in which both parties
hold their arms straight the
entire time.

**The "I'm holding a bunch of stuff,
but I'll still hug you, I guess" Hug!**
Sometimes you really want to hug
people, but you're holding a
bunch of stuff. This hug helps
make that possible.

The Headlock Hug!
Not recommended unless you are
hugging someone who knows you
mean them no harm. Do not use on
professional wrestlers unless you are
also a professional wrestler.

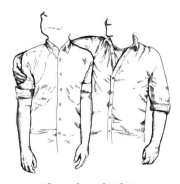

The Awkward Side Hug!
A hug in which one person
does not want to be hugged,
moves to avoid the hug, but
still gets hugged.

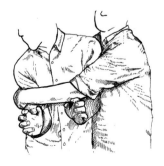

The Awkward Side Bear Hug!
A hug in which a bear does not want to be
hugged, moves to avoid the hug, but still
gets hugged. It should again be noted that
bears do not understand hugs.

**The "I love this book so much,
I have to hug it!" Hug!**
It's okay. Take a moment to hug
this book. We'll wait.

#21

If you see spinach (or anything else) in somebody's teeth, tell them, but only after you've told them something embarrassing about yourself

A great way to help other people be okay with their embarrassing moments is letting them know they're not alone. It's a great equalizer. We've all had embarrassing moments: unzipped pants, toilet paper on our shoe, forgetting you're on live TV and Al Roker wants you to dance with him.

I think you should tell everybody about that girl who liked you.

That was third grade, man. It was a long time ago.

I just think it's funny she called you "Pee-Wee."

I wish I had never told you that.

I'm sorry. I won't bring it up again.

Thank you.

No problem, Pee-Wee.

Going on national live TV can be really exciting, but it can also be really scary and stressful. Especially if you're only 9. Our first TV experience with the cast of the *Today* show was kind of embarrassing because we forgot what to say and both froze, but you just embrace it, laugh, and keep going.

#22

we need to live in a world WITH FEWER SELFIES and more OTHERPEOPLIES

Robby, you love to take selfies. Don't you?

Guilty.

Pretty much any time I leave my phone lying around, I come back to it and find you've taken over 100 photos of yourself.

Ha-ha-ha-ha.

It's funny … at first. Then it gets old.

Nope. It's always funny.

It's important to feel confident in who you are. It's also important to document important moments in your life. (See "Brain Pictures" on page 44.) We're not totally against selfies. But we're aiming for a world with fewer selfies and more otherpeoplies.

Making your life about otherpeoplies means helping other people look good. In doing this you'll come to realize it's more awesome to help other people feel awesome. It means helping celebrate somebody other than yourself. It means spending more time letting other people know how liked they are instead of worrying about your own likes. You'll come to love yourself more and realize you have the power to make awesome things happen in the world.

If everybody just focused on selfies, we'd live in a sad world for sure.

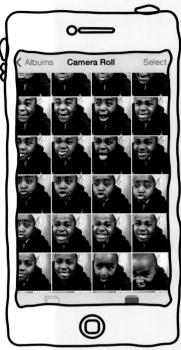

Take more photos with friends. Take more photos with family. Create more moments when people aren't alone. Put your talents to use and make something cool happen for somebody else. You'll be glad you did.

As we look back on the scrapbook of our lives, we'll realize our photos tell a story. They could tell a story of someone who focused just on themselves. This would be a scrapbook with some happy moments, for sure, but overall it would be a pretty sad story. On the other hand, these photos could tell the story of someone who made life awesome for other people. This would be a scrapbook worth celebrating.

Above
Robby really does this with people's phones. The most we have counted was from when he grabbed a friend's phone and took 290 selfies.

How can you spend more time loving and celebrating other people?

#23 PRACTICE the ART of the UNEXPECTED Burrito

Want to surprise your friend with a tasty gift? Your friend's not a fan of surprise corndogs, like in #18? (Don't worry, you can still be friends with them.) Try the "unexpected burrito."

Step 1: Get a burrito.
Step 2: Hide the burrito.
Step 3: Wait for them to find it.

> Um. Wait. Are you sure? What if they don't find it?
>
> They'll find it when it starts smelling.
>
> This isn't a good idea.
>
> Okay. We'll give them a map.

Step 1: Get a burrito.
Step 2: Hide the burrito.
Step 3: Provide a map for your friend to find the burrito so it doesn't get old and smell bad and stuff.

> I like that better.
>
> Yeah, yeah. Whatevs.

You ARE HERE

burrito!

#24 RECOGNIZE

REAL

BEAUTY

MADISON HILL, a longtime pageant participant, found herself bothered by the fact that some people are overlooked by traditional beauty pageants. So she created the Miss Fabulous Pageant, a beauty pageant designed for women and men with special needs.

Growing up, Madison had a heart for those with special needs. "I realized that those with special needs are often overlooked in our community. And God put it on my heart to make a change." By marrying her two interests, she believed she could show special needs individuals that they were worthy of celebration. A pageant would be a chance for young men and women to show off their special talents—for men to feel handsome and girls to feel beautiful—and for the audience to appreciate true beauty.

"A night in the pageant allows the contestants to get their hair and makeup done," Madison says, "or put on a nice tux. It gives them a chance to be cheered on while walking across a stage. It also builds their confidence. After each girl is given a crown, they light up."

Over the years the pageant has grown. The first year, which Madison helped orchestrate when she was 15, they had 38 participants; most recently, they had 120. One of Madison's favorite stories from the pageant involves a young woman named Heather. "The second pageant we had there was a contestant named Heather who decided to enter that year. She was beyond sweet but you could tell that she was shy and nervous about going onstage. I offered to walk with her onstage but she said no and that her daddy would be escorting her. She did an amazing job and she had a blast. So this past year at the third pageant, Heather entered again. But this year, she wanted to walk across the stage all by herself. She not only walked onstage by herself, but she also performed a talent of singing. She did a beautiful job and she had the whole crowd cheering."

But the Miss Fabulous Pageant doesn't just encourage the participants. Everyone involved, from the volunteers to the audience members, are able to celebrate true beauty. Additionally, proceeds from the event are donated to local charities in Madison's community.

At the end of the night, each participant is awarded a sash or a crown. Everyone is a winner. "Everyone deserves to be in the spotlight," she says. "There is beauty all around us and we should all take the time to recognize that. Simple acts of kindness, small conversations, or even a simple smile can bring out the true beauty in people, and that is a beautiful thing."

MADISON HILL
Tennessee, USA

Why She's Awesome:
- She started a pageant for special needs men and women.
- She donated the Miss Fabulous proceeds to charity.
- She believes in seeing the true beauty in everyone.

#25 CELEBRATE somebody's birthday by celebrating other people

This is our friend Matt. He didn't get Brad a present for his birthday last year. Terrible friend, right? Actually, he's an awesome friend! Instead of purchasing a gift, he did something cooler. He and his daughters went out with two dozen cupcakes, handed them out to people, and told them they were celebrating their friend. All day Brad received surprise text messages with stories and photos of people enjoying cupcakes all because he was born.

While it's always cool to get gifts from your friends, it's even cooler to remind them that they are worth celebrating. Find a way to celebrate your friend by celebrating other people. It's a great way to let somebody know that you appreciate them and also spread love.

THIS IS OUR FRIEND MATT

Above
A bunch of strangers enjoy cupcakes to celebrate Brad!

Meet Zach Vanderslice. Instead of having a regular birthday party he had a "Be Awesome" party inspired by Kid President! He asked his friends to help him do something awesome for his big day by inviting them to bring school supplies for kids who needed them. This resulted in 19 backpacks filled with paper, pencils, folders, and more!

A Note from Zach's Mom:

Zach started talking to us about Kid President early last year. His math teacher introduced KP to Zach and his classmates, and Zach was hooked. KP is wise beyond his years—and so funny. He reaches out to kids and connects with them in a way that no parent or other adult really can. Zach was instantly inspired to go out and do something to make a difference in the world, and he particularly seemed to connect with the idea of helping children whose families have suffered financial need.

He was relentless, constantly asking if he could DO something. We had lots of excuses—mostly centered around our general "busyness"—but Zach kept asking and asking. When we really stopped to think about it, we couldn't resist. We had to make time to help Zach BE AWESOME!

Zach did a great job, and we found that he had so much support. All of his communities chipped in. One neighbor, a professional DJ, donated his services to help the kids, all from various communities, come together to "get their groove on." Another neighbor, a social worker in the Richmond Public Schools,

offered the perfect event and helped distribute the donated school supplies. All of Zach's friends and their families donated SO GENEROUSLY that it brought me to tears. With everyone's help, the party was a HUGE success, and Zach could not have been more proud of his efforts.

People can be so good, and so generous, when they have the right motivation and inspiration. Kids like Zach seem to bring that out in even the most philanthropically weary adults. I'm really proud of Zach and all of his friends for coming together to help their community in a truly awesome way.

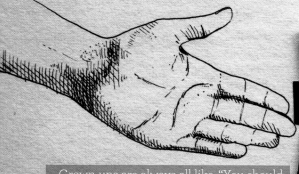

#26
TWO WORDS:
"SHARE"

Just kidding.
That's just one word.
But seriously.
Share.

Grown-ups are always all like, "You should share!" "Are you sharing?" "Be nice! Share!"

You're saying this like it makes you mad.

It does!

You can even share this book with somebody. Do it!

Why? You don't like to share?

I'm fine with sharing. I just think grown-ups should share, too.

That's a really great point. Grown-ups should share. Sometimes we all need to be reminded to do some of the things we teach young children to do.

I know. I'm like, "Give me the car keys. Come on! Share!"

Okay. No. I was following you up until that. I thought you were actually making a really good point. You really just want my car keys.

Come on, man. Share!

That sounds like a terrible idea.

(#27) Sacrifice.

Let someone else have the toy in the cereal.

#28

BE
SOMEBODY
who makes
EVERYBODY
FEEL LIKE A
SOMEBODY

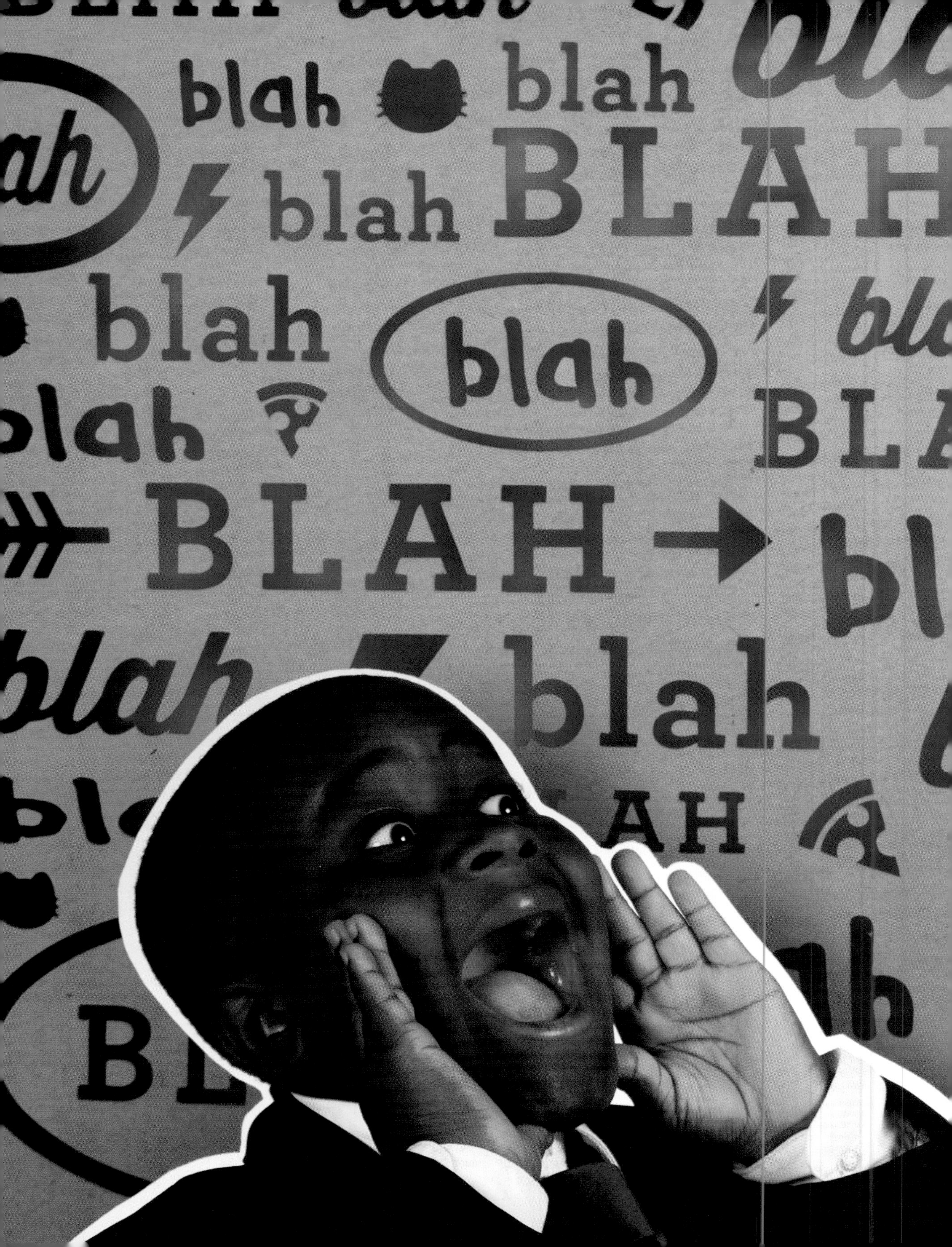
blah
blah
blah
blah
blah
BLAH
blah

CHAPTER 4:
TALK
Gooder!

#29
TALK GOODER

The average person says around 16,000 words in a day. That's a lot of chances to make the world more awesome. Here are a few ideas of things we should all say more often. Remember: Boring people just talk. Awesome people *do*. So don't just talk about saying the things on this list—say them!

20. "Thank you."
This is important not just to say on Thanksgiving. Say it every day.

19. "Excuse me."

18. "Here's a surprise corndog I bought you because you're my friend."
Just imagine it. We'd live in a world with more corndogs and more happy people. A corndog for you, a corndog for you, a corndog for you!

17. "I'm sorry."

16. "I forgive you."

15. "You can do it!"
Be careful, though. Don't say it if it's something they can't do. (Like fly.)

14. "I have barbecue sauce on my shirt, too."
Before you say something about the barbecue sauce on somebody else's shirt, take a look at the barbecue sauce on your own shirt.

13. "Please."

12. "Everything is going to be okay."

11. "Aw! You got me a corndog, too? You shouldn't have, buddy!"
This is something that will hopefully get said more in the world once more
people say #18 more. All these things are connected, man!

You do know she'll be reading this book, right?

Uh-oh.

Just say #17. "I'm sorry."

This list is hard.

10. "I don't know."
I know a lot of people who need to say that.
Ahem . . . my sister!

9. "You're so awesome I named my dog after you." Wait, that could hurt somebody's feelings. I mean boat! **"I named my boat after you."** Wait, who even has a boat? I'm changing it. We should all say, **"You're so awesome, I legally changed my name to yours."** Wait, that's super creepy. Just tell people they're awesome. Say it and mean it!

8. "Hello, person I've never met before. Here's a high five!"

7. "My sports team is not always the best sports team."
This one is extra tough. It takes a big person to say that.

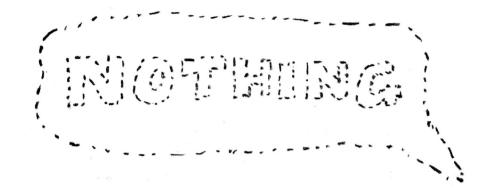

6. "Nothing."
Sometimes this really is the best thing you can say.

5. "Pfft!"
This doesn't really mean anything, but we just think fart noises are funny.

4. "I disagree with you, but I still like you as a person who is a human being, and I will treat you like that because if I didn't, it would make everything bad, and that's what lots of people do, and it's lame."
Phew. It's a mouthful, but maybe we should all say this more. Think about it. We don't all have to agree. It's okay to disagree. It's not okay to be mean.

3. Sometimes you just gotta scream! AAAAAH!

2. "Life is tough, but so are you."
Sometimes we all need to be
reminded to keep going!

1. Something nice! Anything.
If you can't think of anything nice to
say, you're not thinking hard enough.

BONUS IDEAS

BONUS!
"Let's dance."
If people said this more, the world would be less boring and
more awesome! There'd be more dancing and less fighting!
Find a way to say it every single day. You'll be glad you did.

BONUS! BONUS!
"I love you."
It seems obvious, but it's actually not something we say
enough. The thing about saying "I love you" is that it's not
just something you say. It's something you live. Handing out
corndogs and high fives and taking care of people are all
different ways of saying "I love you." So don't just say it. Live it.

#30

Listen

(more than you talk)

If you really want to talk gooder, it's important to remember to listen gooder, too. The things you say are important, but stop and listen more. You might learn something. In fact, you *will* learn something. You might learn that words like "gooder" aren't actually words.

> Wait . . . what?

> It's not a word. It's actually really terrible grammar, buddy.

> You could've told me!

> I did. You didn't hear me.

Right
Robby on the set of *Kid President: Declaration of Awesome*

Opposite Top
Kid President with Uzo Aduba.

Opposite Center
Christina Applegate gives Kid President advice on being cool.

Opposite Bottom
Kid President interviews Nicolas Cage on the red carpet at *The Croods* premiere.

A FEW AWESOME THINGS WE'VE LEARNED FROM LISTENING TO SOME OF OUR FRIENDS:

"They matter, and we listen."
—UZO ADUBA
after being asked what she thinks kids need to know

"You have to go out and talk to people. Everybody has a different perspective. Everybody has a different experience. I think in order to make changes, you have to find out what the different needs are for different people."
—CARRIE BROWNSTEIN

"I think being cool is not about your look; it is about who you are."
—CHRISTINA APPLEGATE

"They are the future of this country and their ideas and their passions are very important to people like us [adults]."
—JESSE TYLER FERGUSON after being asked what he thinks kids need to know

"Try new things. Explore. Experience."
—NICOLAS CAGE

"I guess I got it naturally from inside of my face."
—PEN WARD, creator of *Adventure Time*, responds to Kid President's question about where he got his beard

"What counts is not what they think, but what they do. People must do and not only think about it."
—PAULO COELHO on changing the world

#31 ASK QUESTIONS

What time is it? Where is the bathroom? How do you throw away a garbage can? These are all good questions! Don't be afraid to ask questions. **One question we've been asking a lot is this:**

THE WORLD WOULD BE

Our famous friends had some interesting answers to this question!

"Everybody didn't take themselves too seriously."
—JEREMY LIN

"Everybody laughed more."
—THOMAS LENNON

"All of us could stand in someone else's shoes."
—PATRICK STEWART

"We weren't so afraid to love."
—LUPITA NYONG'O

"I were president! No, just kidding. If you [Kid President] were president one day."
—MICHAEL KELLY

"We all wanted to make a positive difference and a change in the world and loved each other and helped each other."
—JENNIFER HUDSON

"Every interview were as good as this one with Kid President."
—MACKLEMORE

Just about every single interview you've done, you have asked people to help you finish this sentence. Why did you ask people this?

I just thought it would be cool to see what people said.

What do people think would be awesome?

Some people said more pizza. Some people said they didn't know. Some people had really big answers.

Do you have any favorites?

Yes. These!

MORE AWESOME if _____.

Fans online answered the question, too!

"Each person had one day a month (month, week, year, every day) where they set out to do acts of kindness!"
—KRISTIN

"If people were more curious."
—CHARA

"People greeted each other with a friendly 'Hello.' Smiling is contagious."
—HANSEN

"We treated others like they would like to be treated!"
—FREDA

"All the raindrops were lemondrops and gumdrops."
—ALISON

"Everybody danced!"
—LINDSAY

"PIZZA."
—XANDER

How would you answer that question?

#32 Stand in SOMEONE ELSE'S SHOES (metaphorically)

JULIA STILES is a longtime fan of Kid President, and we're a fan of hers, too. We asked her about acting, and about the benefits of putting yourself in other people's shoes.

When did you know you wanted to be an actress?
The first time I stepped onstage.

Do you think pretending to be other people helps you understand other people better?
It requires seeing from different perspectives, empathy, and the ability to find commonality, so yeah.

What are some things people can do to live with more empathy?
In any given interaction, I try to think about where a person is coming from. Literally, what their day was like before we crossed paths. You never know what someone is dealing with before you came into the picture. I worked with an actor who said, "We are all just little souls." I try to remember that. And when someone is being particularly trying, I imagine what they looked like as a toddler.

Putting yourself in someone else's shoes is hard. How do you get over it being so uncomfortable?
I actually don't think it's hard. If a part is well written, it's usually written with empathy, so my job is halfway done. The key to storytelling, in movies, TV, or onstage is to find the commonality, the humanity. "The villain is the hero of his own story," so even if you are playing a monster, you have to find a way to ease up on the judgment.

What's been the best day of your life so far?
I was upstate working outside all day. We were helping a friend who had been growing vegetables, so all day, we were pulling up giant zucchini and squash in the hot sun. It was a day of really muddy overalls. Then the sun went down, and we ate potato chips. It was so simple, but so satisfying.

When you were a kid, what was the best advice you can remember being given?
"How dare you not shine as brightly as you can!" (That's paraphrased.)

Do you have any embarrassing stories from when you were a kid?
I don't think I realized what being embarrassed feels like until I became an adult.

If there were a movie or play written about your life, what do you think the title would be?
Oh, the Places You'll Go. Oops, that's already a title.

Finish this sentence: The world would be more awesome if ___ .
. . . Kid President were 35.

#33 leave notes COMPLIMENTING PEOPLE on how well they parked

People are often quick to leave notes on others' vehicles to let them know they are unhappy with the way they parked, but each and every day there are drivers who heroically park beautifully. These masterful parking jobs go unrewarded. Let a driver know you've been looking for awesome today and you found it when you saw the way they parked.

While you're at it, there are plenty of other ways you can compliment people on things that normally don't get complimented.

Here are a few examples:

Socks. Take a moment to compliment someone on their taste in socks.

Elbows. You don't hear enough good things about elbows these days.

Kneecaps. Much like our elbows, our kneecaps often go unappreciated. Take a moment and let somebody know his or her kneecaps are wonderfully symmetrical.

Lack of a Mustache. Oftentimes, people will compliment someone's mustache, but more should be said of someone's lack of a mustache.

Wait . . . are you just saying this because you really want a mustache and can't grow a mustache?

Not cool, man. And yes.

I love your lack of a mustache. It's great.

Thank you.

#34

Connect
with
people

HOW TO MAKE A CAN PHONE

You don't have to talk to people face-to-face or by phone or using the internet. We've found that one of the best ways to talk to people is via can phone. Somehow, this age-old technology, invented by kids, has a way of making people loosen up and remember what it's like to be a kid.

Step 1. Start with a normal tin can. You'll want to clean it out thoroughly first. (Our first can phones were old cans of cat food and weren't properly cleaned. We regretted this daily.)

Step 2. Find yourself some yarn or string of any length. (Longer is our preference.)

Step 3. Have a grown-up puncture the bottom of the tin can (or cans) just enough to allow for string to be attached.

Step 4. Gather your friends, rations, and satchels as you begin your quest to throw the can into the volcanic depths of Mount Doom. This is what provides the can with its magic.

That last one is very similar to *The Lord of the Rings* and in no way resembles how I remember making our can phones.

You need to get your memory checked.

#35
ASK PEOPLE
IF THEY REMEMBER
BEING A KID

BRAD →

We live in a world where we all have lots of things that divide us. We have differences of opinion, style, and more. It's often easy to forget that there are also many things we have in common, including one big one: At one time, we were all kids.

You've gotten to interview so many really incredible people.

Everybody is awesome, man.

That is true. Who are some of your favorites?

Everybody is awesome.

You're a true politician. One question I love that you've been asking people is . . .

. . . the kid question.

Yeah! You've been asking, "Were you ever a kid?"

It's funny, because of course they were a kid, but I just like asking it.

What have you learned about people from asking this question?

Well, for one thing, everybody at one time was a kid. They always laugh, and then they have a funny story or picture.

Do you have any favorites?

Jeremy Lin showed me a picture of him dressed up as Bambi. It was pretty funny to see a big basketball player as a little person dressed as a baby deer.

That one is great. I also loved your reaction to seeing Mario Lopez's baby photo.

Mario Lopez had the best little chubby baby legs ever! (laughs uncontrollably)

What about talking to First Lady Michelle Obama about her childhood? How was that?

She was really cool and talked about spending time with her family, being active, and playing outside. She also told me about how her dad taught her to box. That was awesome.

It's nice to remember that everybody at one time used to be a little person, right?

Yeah. It makes people not so scary.

#36
MAKE LAUGHTER YOUR OFFICIAL LANGUAGE

Our friend **MONIQUE COLEMAN** is an actress and found[er] of GimmeMo.org, an online talk show and website dedicat[ed] to empowering today's youth. We asked her what makes k[ids] awesome, and here is what she sent us.

Dear Kid President:

Kids are awesome because:

- They inspire us to believe in our dreams.
- They know that what really matters in life is hugs, animals, kindness, friendship, and love!
- For kids, words like "can't," "don't," and "stop" are the real bad words.
- Kids don't declare wars (except the occasional thumb war, which is harmless).
- Their official language is laughter.
- They believe in things that they can't see but know are real.
- Kids look beyond race, religion, and ethnicity to recognize that we're all connected.
- They remind us that life is precious, play is important, and art, dance, and music make the world better.
- They color outside the lines, can turn anything into a toy, and feel lots of feelings.
- Kids are awesome because we are awesome, and if we look deep enough, we'd see that we are all still kids.

I believe with all my heart that we should try to be more like kids instead of making them more like us! Let's listen to their concerns, learn from their wisdom, and be inspired by their imagination. When we empower kids, we change the world. There's more JOY, more HOPE, more POSSIBILITY. Kids aren't who we were; they're who we could be!

Kid Ideas + Kid Leadership + Kid Lunches = Awesomesauce!

Sincerely,
Mo'

CHAPTER 5:
Wanna Be a World Changer? Be a Day Maker!

#37

If you want to be
    a world changer
    for people everywhere,
BE A DAY MAKER FOR THE
PEOPLE RIGHT NEXT to YOU

Changing the world is a big goal. It's crazy big. It's not exactly something you can put on your daily planner and cross off your list at the end of the day.

☒ CHANGE THE WORLD
I did it! Next!

Nope. The world is changed in little pieces every single day. It's all the little things we do daily that add up to something really big. You might think it takes lots of money or power to change the world, but those aren't the secret. The key to changing the world is love. It's little acts of love you spread wherever you are that make a big difference.

It's sort of like that guy who ate that airplane.

What do you mean?

There's this guy who ate an airplane. It took him a few years but he did it. Just little bits at a time.

But why?

I guess he was hungry. He ate an entire airplane.

How do you know about this?

A kid at school told me. He said it really happened, but he says lots of things.

Well, this is, I guess, sort of like that guy eating an airplane, except being a day maker is actually good for you.

. . . and all the people around you.

Yes, definitely better for everybody.

Opposite
The amazing view from the top floor of the United Nations building, outside the Secretary General's office.

Top
Robby contemplating the world on the set of *Kid President: Declaration of Awesome.*

Bottom
Fan art by Emelina Spinelli from New York.

Take a moment to think of ways you can make today more awesome for somebody next to you. Imagine a world where everybody decided to make the day for the person next to them better. If we all did that, then the whole world would be taken care of. Sound like a plan? Go be a day maker.

Whose day can you make more awesome today?

#38

SEND A CARD. EVERY DAY. FOR 365 DAYS.

— KP

You don't have to have a reason. It doesn't have to be a holiday. You can make every day a holiday. In case you're looking for an excuse to send a card, here are a few ideas:

- *I was thinking of you. Here's a card!*
- *It's "You Deserve a Card" Day. Here's a card!*
- *You inspire me. Here's a card!*
- *Congratulations on not falling down yesterday. Here's a card!*
- *Your dog is cool. Here's a card!*
- *Where did you get your shoes? I need to know. Here's a card!*
- *I picked a random address in the phone book and liked your name. Here's a card!*
- *I had too many stamps. Here's a card!*
- *You were asking me yesterday for a card. Here's a card!*
- *Sorry I misspelled a word in my email. Here's a card!*
- *Happy "Day after Groundhog Day"! Here's a card!*
- *It's three weeks after your birthday! Here's a card!*
- *You sent me a thank you card. Here's a thank you card from me thanking you for your thank you card!*
- *Space Jam was on TV, and I thought you should know. It's too late for you to watch it now, though. In retrospect, I probably should have texted you. Oh well. Here's a card!*

#39 BE CONFIDENT.
IT'S CONTAGIOUS.

NICK HORNBY is a pretty famous writer whose books include *About a Boy* and *High Fidelity*. And he wants kids to write more and share their ideas. Here's what he told us about writing.

You're a big deal writer. What if my book has misspelled words or misplaced commas?

Well, you emailed me. That means you must have access to a computer. And that means you have spell-check and all sorts of tools to help you. Some people probably get too upset about mistakes, and that's annoying, especially if mistakes are the first things they notice, rather than the jokes or truth or smartness.

What made you want to grow up and become a writer?

I don't know if I wanted to be a writer, but I do know that I didn't really seem to have a choice. I was convinced that it was the only real talent I had, even before I'd ever written anything. So I wrote and wrote, and eventually publishers just gave in and let me be a published writer.

What's the big deal about stories? Why should the world read them?

Stories are important to us. When we come home from work or school, we tell our families stories. I don't mean we sit them down and start going on about tortoises and hares or Cinderella, I mean that when we talk about our days, we try and shape the anecdotes, give them beginnings and middles and ends. Stories are a pretty good way of talking about the world and making sense of it.

Tell me about what you're doing to help kids with the Ministry of Stories.

The Ministry of Stories is a literacy center in London, England, for kids between the ages of 8 and 18. Teachers bring classes in, and the class gets together and writes a story, and they leave with a finished book with their name on it. We stole everything, all of it, the idea for the tutoring center, from my friend Dave Eggers, who founded the 826 schools in America. Don't tell Dave we stole the idea, though.

What have you learned from helping with the Ministry of Stories?

So many things are about confidence. Sometimes it seems as though you can divide the world up into two sets of people—the confident and the unconfident. And confident people can do so much more. We're trying to give kids confidence by introducing them to confident grown-ups. There are lots of kids, especially kids in poorer neighborhoods, who never get the chance to hang out with people who have the confidence to get things done. Confidence is contagious.

How can people live a better story?

That's a smart question. Do you know what a cliché is, Kid President? It's a part of a story that's been used too many times already, so there's nothing left in it. Writers are trying to avoid clichés all the time. Well, we all should. The guy who works too hard and doesn't pay any attention to his wife and kids—that's a cliché. The kid who drops out of school and gets involved with bad people—that's another cliché. If we can avoid clichés in the narratives of our own lives, then we'll do well. You can live happily ever after, though. The phrase is a cliché, but the idea is fine.

Finish this sentence: The world would be more awesome if _____.

Every time people felt angry with themselves or someone else, they listened to the whole of Paul Simon's *There Goes Rhymin' Simon* before carrying on with their lives.

#40 Find Your :Light: (AND SHARE IT)

JOSH GROBAN is a world-famous singer, songwriter, and all around nice guy. When we first started doing our web show he posted online about being a big fan. We were so excited and tried to reach out to him to thank him and invite him to be on it. When we didn't hear from him we did a special episode where we urged our audience to #BugJoshGroban. Several thousand tweets and just two hours later we heard back from him! Not only did we get to do an interview, we got to find out what an awesome dude he really is.

Sorry about that time I got the entire internet to bug you. You're not still mad, are you?

How could I be mad? Because you commanded the internet to bug me I found out more about you and your awesome message and now we're friends! I wish all the bugging in the world was for such good things. Mostly it's just to borrow car keys or five bucks.

You're really into music. Why is music awesome?

Music is awesome because it's a language EVERYONE speaks. You can say things to someone with music that words could never say. Music is awesome because it gets people out of their heads and gets them feeling and not just thinking. I think it could truly solve most of the world's problems.

One thing you do that is awesome is you help kids through the Find Your Light Foundation. What is it?

It's probably the most awesome thing I've been lucky enough to do! It's a foundation that I started with my fans to bring music and the arts into the lives of young people. You and I are lucky that we get to express ourselves all the time, but a lot of kids don't get that chance. Find Your Light is all about giving them a voice they haven't had before.

What makes you want to keep helping kids find their "light"?

It's important because your generation is going to change the world. And I think the arts are an important way to teach about love, tolerance, expression, and understanding of many different cultures and worldviews. There will always be differences in the world, but the arts is something we all share within us. It's the great connector!

Who are some people who encouraged you when you were a kid?

I was so fortunate to have great teachers and great parents who saw my love of music and nurtured it and allowed me the opportunities to try. I had a teacher who could see I had a good voice but I was shy. He pulled me out from the back of the choir in 7th grade and gave me a solo. I never looked back!

Finish this sentence: The world would be more awesome if _____.

Music were a language taught in every school in the world.

(#41) Be cool
to people even if
they're not cool
to you, because
somebody was
probably NOT COOL
to them

#42 Paint A Park Bench

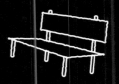

CHRISTIAN BUCKS is a 3rd grader in York, PA. One day, he noticed something that made him sad: Some of his elementary school classmates had no one to play with during recess. So he came up with a solution—the Buddy Bench.

The Buddy Bench sounds pretty cool.
What is it exactly?
The Buddy Bench is a new way to make friends. I knew there were kids who were lonely and that made me sad because they deserve to have friends, too. A Buddy Bench is a special bench on a playground, usually with a special sign or brightly painted. If you are feeling lonely at recess and don't have anyone to play with, you go sit on the bench. Someone will see you sitting on the bench and ask you if you want to play or talk. If two people sit on the bench, they can play or talk together.

What was the response when you first set it up?
Kids at my school were really excited and happy about it!

Are there any stories that have come out of setting up the Buddy Bench at your school or another school?
One of my favorite stories is from a student in California. He was so unhappy at his school that he wanted to leave it and be homeschooled. His mom showed him the Buddy Bench story on the internet, and he took action! He talked to his principal about it and was able to get one at his school. Now he is the happiest he has ever been at school!

Why do you think the Buddy Bench works?
I think the Buddy Bench works because kids want to be kind and include one another. The Buddy Bench gives them a little reminder when they might get wrapped up in recess activities. Also, it is something that is really easy to do.

How can people fight loneliness and spread kindness?
They can just be aware of including kids around them and look out for someone who needs a friend. A friendly smile or saying, "Hey, do you want to sit with me?" can go a really long way!

Finish this sentence: The world would be more awesome if _____.
More big people listened to the ideas of little people and worked with them to make them happen!

CHRISTIAN BUCKS
Pennsylvania, USA

Why He's Awesome:
- He created the Buddy Bench to help classmates combat loneliness at recess.
- He used his creativity to change his world, with the help of grown-ups.
- Matt Lauer called him his "new favorite kid."

#43 ASK YOUR BEST FRIEND FOR HELP

There are some kids who only eat when they're in school. Which means they don't eat dinner or have meals on the weekends. When best friends **CATLYN WATKINS** and **ADDISON POINTER** were 18, they heard this and decided to work together to start a monthly program called Handy Lunches in their Alabama neighborhood to help those kids.

What inspired you to create Handy Lunches?

It was our senior year of high school, and we were in charge of the canned food drive at school. Seeing the few families we were able to help made us want to do something on a larger scale to help as many as we could. So we created Handy Lunches, which is a free meal program every second Saturday of the month. When we had the idea, we started with a lot of talking, thinking, and praying. Then we started talking to others to get ideas the best way to do it. And after that, we went to our church for help. We have it at the community center, which is in walking distance of most of the people that we serve.

Was it tough to do the first few times?

The first one, we were just running on adrenaline. We were just amazed that we had 40 people come to eat and we didn't have panic attacks. But there has never been a Handy Lunches that is the same. So we learn something new every time we have it—maybe it's a better way to organize something or about the people that come in or even something about ourselves.

Why is a program like Handy Lunches important?

Fulfilling the physical needs with food or clothes are good, but just showing love to those that might not have any in their life is important. And for us, sometimes that part is hard to remember. We get focused on the organizing and getting the food served. And that's usually when God puts someone there to remind us what it's about.

What advice can you give to someone who wants to help?

If you see a need, just know that you don't have to do anything big and scary. Anyone can start something similar. You just have to make sure you're ready to be committed, and not be scared to ask anyone and everyone around you for help and to get involved. Start with a lot of praying, and then think of some ideas on how to help. It's okay to have lots and lots of ideas and know that some of them might work and some might not, and that's okay. You have to remember it's not all fluffy and great all the time, but don't let that stop you!

Finish this sentence: The world would be more awesome if _____.

We would not dwell on things we can't change and work on the things we can.

CATLYN WATKINS & ADDISON POINTER
Alabama, USA

Why They're Awesome:

- They have done monthly Handy Lunches programs for more than a year.
- They expanded their program to start collecting donations for shoes, coats, and other basic necessities.
- They're best friends, and they both have pretty cool names.

#44 INVENT A NEW HANDSHAKE

Want to really connect with the people directly next to you? Create a secret handshake, and let them in on it. Make your friendships more awesome by mixing and matching elements from these handshakes or invent your own!

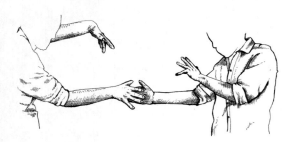

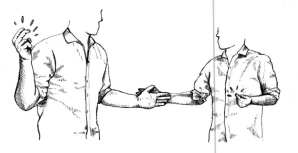

The Overly Complicated Bro Shake!

The key here is to add in elements that are distinct to you and the fellow owner of this secret handshake. You will want it to have several steps so that people watching can't easily decipher all the pieces and steal it for themselves. Spice it up with a few animal noises for additional flavor.

The Snap, Crackle, Plop Shake!

This handshake fools those looking on by beginning as a normal handshake but morphs quickly into something much more powerful. After the initial shake, both parties snap their fingers, move their fingers while making crackling noises, and then fall down.

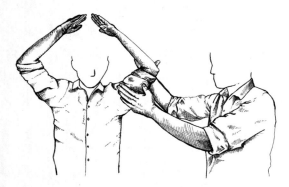

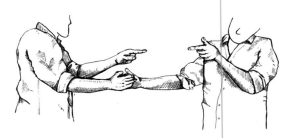

The "I Think Those Two People Are Hurt—No, Wait, I Think It's Just a Weird Secret Handshake" Shake!

This involves lots of large hand gestures and motions incorporating elements from ballet, action cinema, and air traffic controllers.

The "We're Making It Up as We Go, But It Sort of Looks Like We Know What We're Doing" Shake!

This is a classic and one of the most utilized. It allows both parties to act as though they know the handshake from years of friendship, but actually are both faking it. Sometimes it can be uncertain if either participant knows exactly what handshake is happening, but it does always end with a knowing glance, giving whatever has transpired a nice end point.

#45 Solve a conflict using ICE CREAM!

Take two people who are in disagreement about something. Put them in a room. Have them talk about what they disagree on. There might be shouting, but let it go for a moment. Now, give them each ice cream. Have the two discuss how much they both love ice cream. Now that common ground has been found, they can proceed to find a solution together. Congratulations, you've just solved a conflict using ice cream.

Note: Please be aware of any lactose intolerance beforehand, as this could cause your peace project to backfire.

In 2008, **KATIE STAGLIANO** started Katie's Krops, an organization that donates crops to those in need. We talked to her about gardening, her organization, and a 40-pound cabbage.

What do you think awesome looks like?
I think awesome is a world where there is no hunger, a world where nobody goes to bed hungry, and everybody eats a well-balanced diet!

When did you first fall in love with gardening?
I started to really love gardening after I grew my 40-pound cabbage. I realized how much fun it was and how by gardening I could help make a difference in the world.

You've said your dream is that there would be no hungry people. How can it come true?
I believe we can end hunger by empowering youth. Over the course of a year, our flagship garden has over 450 youth volunteers come and help tend to it, and over the course of a year, our flagship garden yields over 3,000 pounds of fruits and vegetables. If we used this model, and empowered kids to make a difference on an even bigger scale, imagine what could happen!

What's been the most exciting thing for you as you've started Katie's Krops?
One of the most exciting things for me has been seeing how many other kids are as passionate about ending hunger as I am. When I first started offering grants to other kids 4 years ago, I didn't think anybody would apply. However, that first grant cycle, I received over 200 applications! I was amazed at how many kids are as passionate about ending hunger as I am.

What are some things you've done to get people involved in helping to fight hunger?
I started hosting monthly dinners in my community after the only soup kitchen in my area shut its doors due to lack of funding. Once a month, my friends and I come together to create healthy, fresh meals with the produce from the gardens that is free to anyone in need in the community.

What advice do you have for kids who want to make the world a better place?
My advice would be to follow your heart. Look for a cause that you truly believe in, and remember, anything is possible! It doesn't matter how small or large your efforts are, every little bit helps. Never let anybody tell you that you can't, because whether you're 9 or 99, you can make a difference in the world.

Finish this sentence: The world would be more awesome if _____.
Hunger didn't exist!

KATIE STAGLIANO
South Carolina, USA

Why She's Awesome:
- She donates produce to the less fortunate.
- She helps run a soup kitchen called Katie's Krops Dinners.
- When she was 9, she grew a 40-pound cabbage (40 pounds!).

GUEST CHECK

Date	Table	Server	01423376

APPETIZER-SOUP/SALAD-ENTREE-CORNDOG-DESSERT-DRINK

#47 TIP BIG, YO

Thank you!

KP   TOTAL

#48 HIGH FIVE *your* DENTIST

We haven't met your dentist but just thought he might love a high five. Also, we wanted to make sure you were still following through with the whole "more high fives" thing. I mean, that was way earlier in the book, but it's still important. We've got a whole world to make awesome, people. Can't leave this stuff out! Proceed.

#49 — DECLARE AN ENTIRE MONTH SOMETHING AWESOME!

Kindness. Generosity. Compassion. These things are contagious.

People want to help. One great way you can make a big difference is by making an effort to focus your time and energy on something you really care about. Take a period of time, set a goal, and then work to make it happen. It doesn't have to be a month. It could be a couple of weeks or even a few days. Just take a block of time and work to make something awesome happen in it.

So take a month and make something awesome! Example:

Yesvember. Take the month of November and make it 4 whole weeks of pushing people to be positive.

A few years ago our family discovered there was a large population of men and women who were homeless living right in our community. We wanted to do something but weren't sure what or how. After talking with a friend who worked at our local homeless shelter, we found there were several things we could do to help make sure these men and women had their basic needs met. One item of

Left
Michelle Labi, California, USA: A high school's news broadcast encourages students to support #Socktober with sock puppets they created (Jacques the Sock and Stan, General Sockman). Their efforts resulted in 800 pairs of new socks for the homeless!

Opposite
Isaac Baker, Arkansas, USA: For his 7th birthday, Isaac Baker asked his friends to be part of Socktober with him. He collected over 300 pairs of socks for the homeless in his community of Searcy, Arkansas.

other basic needs (soap, deodorant, blankets, etc.) for the shelter. Our one little box turned into a few more boxes as local schools and churches began pitching in. This was exciting to see because it became something everyone felt they could take part in.

We found out we weren't alone in wanting to do something for our homeless neighbors. People were looking for a way to help. We even recorded a rap song about socks to help spread the word. The whole thing grew to be something much bigger than us. As October came and went, the project still had life in it. Donations continued to come in, and other initiatives popped up to keep the giving going.

A few years later, after our Kid President videos found their audience online, we decided to see if our new online friends would get in on the action and join in the fun. In the video, we set a goal of getting 1 million people to help their local homeless neighbors. Kid President let people know how they could help make Socktober awesome by collecting items for their shelter, learning a homeless neighbor's name, or donating to build a shelter. (The shelter was being built by our friend Aaron Reddin, who works with homeless men and women in and around Little Rock, Arkansas. Check out the next page for an update!)

specific need the shelter had at that time? Socks.

It was a simple item that we took for granted. It made us think about all the other things we might take for granted that someone living on the streets might need but not have.

We took the month of October and dubbed it Socktober. It started small, with a little box of our own. We set out collecting new socks and

SOCKTOBER IN ACTION!

Our friend Aaron helps his homeless brothers and sisters with a dream, a van . . . and with piles and piles of socks. We asked him to tell his story.

About 4 years ago, I launched a grassroots nonprofit with the mission to locate and love our unsheltered homeless neighbors. Just because some don't own walls doesn't mean they aren't neighbors. We visit camps, bridges, and alleys—wherever folks may be—and strive to build relationships. We all live here. We don't want to see anyone in our community living outside. We want to see everyone around us doing okay. Being okay.

Anyways, about that time, I got an email from a strange dude who said he wanted to sing songs on the internet to get people to donate socks. I had no idea what to think, so I said okay and went about my business. A few weeks later, that same strange dude (his name was Brad) showed up in Arkansas with something like 1,600 pairs of socks for us. We hit it off, and I knew right away that this strange dude was legit!

We connected again before Kid President's Socktober campaign. Brad wanted to team up and help make our dream of opening a homeless shelter—a safe, dry, warm/cool place for homeless women and children—a reality. We have a severe shortage of female shelter beds in our area. Existing shelters are almost always full, so when we're out on the streets and come across a woman or a mom with kids, it's next to impossible to get them in somewhere immediately.

For me, the coolest part was watching the donations come in from literally all over this planet. It was the most insane thing to see people open their hearts and wallets and give to this little grassroots effort in Arkansas. The whole world blew our minds. Almost $25,000 came in for this effort, and we found a house! Since then, we've been working on the paint, plumbing, and electrical. We will be providing immediate hospitality to our homeless ladies before Socktober rolls around again. Um . . . it is gonna roll around again, right? Right?!?

AARON REDDIN
Arkansas, USA

Why He's Awesome:
- His nonprofit, The One, has helped countless women and children get off the streets.
- He battled drugs as a teen and ended up overcoming it by working at a long-term treatment program and homeless shelter.
- He responds to emails from strange guys in Tennessee.

Above Left

JoLisa Hoover, Texas, USA: 4th graders at River Ridge Elementary in Leander, TX, celebrate their sock drive for Socktober.

Above Right

Barbara Rivera, North Carolina, USA: Caleb Rivera collecting socks for the Raleigh Rescue Mission in North Carolina. He was able to get support from local businesses and his school, Bradford Academy. His mother, Barbara, writes, "We plan to do it again this year. It's an awesome opportunity to let kids bless those who have so little."

HOW TO HOLD A SOCKTOBER DRIVE IN YOUR TOWN

Step 1. Start with your neighborhood!

Find out what the needs are in your neighborhood. Gather up socks or other basic essentials your local shelter might need depending on what season they're preparing for. Never connected with your local shelter? You can find one here: homelessshelterdirectory.org

Step 2. Get your friends involved!

This is a perfect project to do as a family, with your school, your workplace, or your next-door neighbors. Post handmade fliers at your school or spread the word on social media. Set a goal. Set a deadline. Make it happen!

Step 3. Deliver the donations!

When your drive is done, it's time to make the deliver to your local shelter! While you're there be sure to look for other ways you could help.

Step 4. Start back at Step 1!

You'll find that helping people is pretty contagious. It doesn't have to end just because the month is up. Keep going!

#50 WRITE LETTERS

SHARON LI is the president of We Care Act. With her sister Grace and her brother Eric, Sharon works to help kids all over the world respond when disaster hits. Their relief efforts started in 2008 when they were just 12, 10, and 7 years old, respectively. What first happened door-to-door in their neighborhood has turned into a global network of kids helping kids.

Sharon, you and your brother and sister started We Care Act. Why?
As a child, I was sheltered from the horrors of the world, but when I was 9 an 8.0 earthquake struck Sichuan, China, causing 90,000 deaths. Grace, Eric, and I cried so much watching the devastating TV footage. We first worried about our grandparents in China. I was relieved to know that my grandparents were not affected, but still the situation there changed my life. It was my first taste of grief and I vowed to do something. With those who aided us, Grace, Eric, and I were able to raise $6,000 within months. We donated our initial funds to the Red Cross and personally delivered $1,500 along with books and homemade bookmarks to 5 children in one of the hardest-hit areas in Dujiangyan, Sichuan, China.

In 2011, Japan was hit by an earthquake and tsunami that left so much devastation and you guys set out to help spread hope. How?
Letters to Japan was definitely one of our most memorable projects. It was our first majorly non-monetary project and the response was overwhelming. Thousands of letters from every corner of the earth; I had to ask my mother how in the world people were even discovering this project.

Any idea how many letters you guys received?
We received a total of 6,749 items, including 5,149 letters and cards and 1,579 origami cranes from students and teachers in 135 schools/organizations from 16 different countries.

What keeps you going, especially when things aren't easy?
When we were first starting We Care Act, it was incredibly difficult to get people to take us seriously. A trio of kids—the oldest not even 12 years old—was not exactly the "dream team" that many would expect. Over and over we would be told that this type of "grown-up work should be left for the adults," but to us, it felt like we were the only ones left for the job. Every smile, every donation, every "good job" and "keep up the hard work" means the world to us. It keeps me going and I'm immensely grateful for those people who donate their kindness if not their funds.

Finish this sentence: The world would be more awesome if _____ .
Everyone was more aware of our world's problems.

SHARON LI
Texas, USA

Why She's Awesome:
- She helped found We Care Act, a non-profit that 1) helps kids recover from disaster, and 2) encourages kids to help others in need.
- She is one of the ten Youth Service America Global Youth Council members selected from around the world.
- She is a nationally recognized poet.

#51 THINK MORE LIKE A KID

When he was in 1st grade, **RYAN HRELJAC** discovered that not everyone had access to water. His foundation, Ryan's Well, began because of the steps he took after he learned that fact.

When did you first learn that not everybody in the world has access to clean water?
I was 6 years old and in 1st grade when I realized the world has a water problem. It just wasn't fair to me that other kids spent their entire days walking miles upon miles for dirty water while I had clean water just 10 steps away, right outside my classroom.

So you set out to build a well, right? What happened next?
I started doing extra chores at home, and told my family, friends, and anyone who'd listen about the world's water crisis so I could raise the $70 I thought would build a well. Turned out I was wrong about the $70. It was going to cost $2,000. So I did more chores and talked to more people. It took me almost a year but I raised enough money to build a well in Uganda.

What was it like to begin to see all your hard work result in real wells and real water?
It taught me a lot. When I was a kid and even now, I like to play sports, sleep in on weekends, and play video games. But my experiences with volunteering have changed my perspective on what I need to be happy. Not to say we should feel guilty about having access to clean water and the luxury to go to school and sleep in on weekends. But what I realized over the years is that it's important to have a balance and give back when you have more than you need.

What advice would you have for any grown-ups out there?
Think more like a kid. The more I look back on when I started, the more I realize how naïve I was. There were a lot of challenges to building even one well, but I was naïve enough to think I could do it and that helped me overcome the challenges. Then I just kept going. When you're a kid, you tend to be more resourceful and don't take "no" as easily as you do when you're older.

What advice would you have for any kids out there who want to change the world?
I think the first step is to find what gets you excited and passionate. And then the second step, which is harder, is to actually do something about it. It doesn't have to be on a grand scale. Just do something. Anything. Because small steps lead to big change. The Ryan's Well foundation is a good example of that. Get your friends and your family to help. Be informed. Show you care. And just go for it!

Finish this sentence: The world would be more awesome if _____.
Everyone had access to clean water.

RYAN HRELJAC
Ontario, Canada

Why He's Awesome:
- He raised millions to help Africans gain access to clean water.
- He started small—he got his start by collecting pocket change.

#52 THINK OF SOMETHING YOU WANT TO SAY, AND THEN SING IT INSTEAD

It's always been our dream to have a hit single. The **GREGORY BROTHERS** helped us get there! "The World Can Be Better" raised money to fight homelessness as part of our Socktober campaign. And it's good. It's *real* good. So we talked to them about the power of music.

Why is music so awesome?
To quote Maria von Trapp, "The hills are alive with the sound of music." That means that music has the power to make a collection of huge, inanimate objects come to life, which is pretty cool and weird. That's how I feel when I listen to music—like a huge pile of bedrock and soil in Austria that just wants to get up and dance.

What's the best song in the world?
"Her Majesty" by the Beatles because they fit an entire song into 23 seconds.

Nope. Wrong. It's actually "Bohemian Rhapsody" by Queen. Is that how music works? Is there right and wrong? This song is the best and this song is not? That sort of thing?
No, there is no right or wrong—some people want pizza and some prefer lo mein. Personally, we like to have spaghetti and meatballs at Uncle Carmen's house because we know he'll make it the best, but after a long kayak ride, it's nice to have a fresh BLT. What was the question?

How do you write songs?
Think of something you want to say, and then sing that instead.

What made you want to team up with me and make a song?
We were glad to help out with Socktober. You inspired us (and a lot of other humans), and we wanted to turn your words into a song we could all dance to. Like jubilant, verdant Austrian hummocks doing the jitterbug.

How has music inspired you in the past?
One time I listened to the Yams from Outer Space while I was cleaning my room and finished 15 minutes faster.

How can creativity make the world more awesome?
Creative people make the world more awesome every day—and you don't have to be a musician or artist to be creative. The creativity of scientists, engineers, teachers, public servants, inventors, and many others can leave behind a better world.

What are the benefits and challenges of making stuff with your family?
Benefits: We have a lot in common (e.g., parents). Challenges: We have a little too much in common (e.g., lack of dishwashing skills).

Finish this sentence: The world would be more awesome if _____.
You know those hats that have drink-holders on the side and plastic tubes that siphon the drink into your mouth? Well, the world would be more awesome if they had those, but for cheeseballs.

#53 Write and record a song for someone

MY AWESOME SONG THAT I WROTE FOR YOU
by me

Chords: C, G, Am, F

You have _____
awesome quality about person here
and you also have _____
something awesome that the person owns here
but why don't you have your own song?

It's not because you haven't _____
something awesome the person has done
and it's not because you haven't _____ .
something awesome the person has done
It's just because I hadn't written your song yet.

But now I'm writing your song
and I think you should take a look.
I didn't write it with fill-in-the-blank help from a book.
I wrote it from the heart.
Totes from the heart.
You are still my friend, even though I say,
"Totes from the heart."

Thank you for _____
something awesome the person has done for you
back when _____ .
the specific time frame the person did the awesome thing for you
It really made me want to write you a song.

So I did.
Oh. Oh.
So I did.
Oh. Oh.

Your hair is _____ .
something about person's hair
And another thing about you is _____ .
something else about the person

I'm writing your song,
and I think you should take a look.
I didn't write it with fill-in-the-blank help from a book.
I wrote it from the heart.
Totes from the heart.
You are still my friend, even though I say,
"Totes from the heart."

You are really cool, _____ .
insert person's name

Want to really let somebody know they're awesome? Write them a song! You don't need fancy gear. Just use whatever you have and write something from the heart. They'll love it. Every superhero needs a theme song, right?

In case you need some help, we've started a song for you.

#54 HELP SOMEBODY WHO IS YOUNGER THAN YOU

It's scary, but it's true: Somebody is learning how to be a person by watching you. There's a lot that kids needs to know, so be awesome and take a moment to share

A LETTER TO A PERSON ON THEIR FIRST DAY HERE

Today, over 360,000 babies will be born and you are one of them. Welcome! This is the world. It's a pretty cool place. There's lots to see and smell. There's corndogs. Uh, I'm getting ahead of myself. There's just so much to do. There's singing and dancing and laughing. It's especially great when you laugh and milk comes out of your nose. Well, it's only great if you just had milk. Otherwise it's just gross, but some days gross things will happen. Some days awesome things will happen.

Some days you'll get ice cream. Some days you won't. Some days your kite will fly high. Some days it gets stuck in a tree. That's just how it is here.

Don't worry, though. You won't be doing this alone. You're going to meet lots of people here. Some of them will be really nice and some won't be. It's not that they can't be nice. It's just—well, maybe they're just having a bad day.

Being a person is hard sometimes. You should give people high fives just for getting out of bed. Treat everybody like it's their birthday, even if they don't deserve it because we all mess up sometimes. The biggest mess-up? Not forgiving each other's mess-ups.

Maybe you'll be a teacher or become president. Maybe you'll cure every disease ever. You might see the Grand Canyon or swim in the ocean.

Oh, this is so, so much. This is a lot. Sorry.

Here. Try this: Take a breath. Isn't that amazing? It's called breathing. You're going to do it a lot, but nobody knows exactly how much. So enjoy it.

Pay attention, because amazing things will happen every day.

You're going to do so much, but it's not about what you do. It's about who you are. And you? You're awesome. You were made that way. You were made from love, to be loved, to spread love, and love is always louder. Even if hate has a bullhorn, love is louder. So let your life be loud! Let it shout to the world: Things can be better! It's okay about all the mess-ups! Corndogs rule! (Sorry about bringing up corndogs again.)

I don't think I told you this yet. We're really glad you're here. We don't say that enough to each other here. Life gets busy. You're going to be important, and you're going to do a lot, but don't get too busy. Remember to let everybody know you're glad they're here.

You don't have to remember all of this right now. You're going to need a pep talk sometimes. And that's okay.

For now, just remember this: You're awake. You're awesome. Live like it.

This letter was written by Brad for a little guy named Miles (his son, Robby's nephew).

#55 READ. THEN READ SOME MORE.

ADELE ANN TAYLOR is the founder of Adele's Literacy Library, an organization that empowers all people to read. We talked to Adele about her love of reading, and about her dream to extinguish illiteracy.

Have you always loved reading?
Yes! My mother always tells the story of how the only way to keep me quiet as a baby was to read. In fact, when I was younger, after I said goodnight to my parents, I would go upstairs in my room, get under the covers, and with a flashlight, finish reading a book. Sometimes I would stay up for hours way past my bedtime. After my parents learned of my late-night readings, they installed mini-lights under my bookshelf, which was the length of my wall and above my bed, which I could use to read at night.

How old were you when you started your mission to help empower people all over the world through reading?
In December 2008, at the age of 13, I created Adele's Literacy Library. Adele's Literacy Library is a not-for-profit, tax-exempt organization that empowers people of ALL ages to read and has empowered over 25,000 people through our initiatives and programs.

What inspired you to do this?
In school, I began to notice some of my classmates struggling with certain words that they should've already comprehended. After telling my mom one day about what I discovered, she asked me what I was going to do about it. With internet research and a passion for literacy I decided to create an organization to spread the importance of literacy.

What's it like to see entire schools built and lives changed?
Having the opportunity to partner with Under the Acacia to aid in the construction of a learning center in Loita, Kenya, that has 20 laptop stations, a reading room, and a library that has the capacity to hold 4,000 books all under solar energy was a dream come true. Through this building, the Massai tribe and its surrounding communities now have access to technology, knowledge, and the internet. Our goal is to continue to look to construct other learning centers in areas with the highest illiteracy rates with the aid of aggressive partnerships and collaborations.

What can people do to help change lives through literacy?
I challenge you to pick up a book that you've been putting off reading, tell someone how important literacy is and why, or even donate your time to read to groups of students or elders. Then, share your literacy challenge with Adele's Literacy Library to be featured on our social media, website, and newsletter. Visit us at www.AdelesLiteracyLibrary.org.

Finish this sentence: The world would be more awesome if _____.
People would follow their dreams and use their passions to help others.

ADELE ANN TAYLOR
New Jersey, USA

Why She's Awesome:
- She decided to help reduce illiteracy rates when she was 13.
- She has empowered over 25,000 to read.
- She is a good punctuator.

CHAPTER 6:

BE A PARTY!

#57
Don't be in a party.
Be a party.

Oh yeah! It's time to be a party! But don't worry if you're not the loudest or wildest person in the room. Being a party isn't about being loud and crazy. It's about making the world awesome everywhere you go just by being who you are. Make everywhere you go a party. If you're doing whatever you can with whatever you have to help the people around you, then you're being a party. When you live your life as a party, it invites people into something they can't help but want to be part of. It invites people to celebrate everywhere you go.

(#58) BE LIKE
Cheese (or bacon)

AND MAKE EVERYTHING
YOU TOUCH *better*

#59 THROW A PARADE!

There are a lot of people all around you who help make your day easier or more awesome. These are everyday heroes. Everyday heroes don't always get the recognition they deserve. They don't do it for the recognition. They do it because they are awesome! Find little and big ways to celebrate them. All it takes is some streamers and flowers and a bunch of friends.

We love the mail lady in our town. Her name is Dana. She's worked at the small post office here for decades and makes it more awesome every day she's worked there. Without fail, she can always brighten your day, no matter how long the line might get.

One day we just decided somebody should do something nice for her. She works so hard and helps so many people and never gets any recognition. It was time somebody let her know what she means to this town. Why not us?

We thought about lots of things: gift cards, a note, a corndog. None of those seemed like the

right fit. This was Dana, after all. She deserved something more. She deserved . . . a parade!

We definitely wanted this to be a surprise, but we couldn't bear the thought of planning this whole thing and risking her not being at work that day. After conspiring with her coworkers to find out what day (and what time of day) might work best for her, we hatched the perfect plan. We then assembled as many people as we could to make the day of the parade one she deserved.

I liked your outfit that day.

Oh, man. I borrowed it. It was an old marching-band uniform from a friend.

You borrowed it from a much smaller friend. Ha-ha-ha.

Yes. It was very tight.

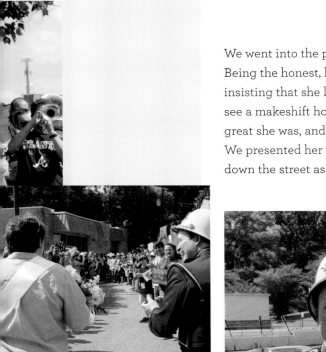

We went into the post office and asked Dana if she would step outside. Being the honest, hardworking woman she is, it took her coworkers insisting that she leave her post. Once she did, she stepped outside to see a makeshift horn section, a variety of handmade signs declaring how great she was, and, in total, a crowd of more than 300 cheering people. We presented her with a sash, a crown, and flowers, and then marched her down the street as she smiled and laughed in disbelief.

Even though Brad's outfit was a little tight, we still managed to throw our friend Dana the best parade ever!

She cried. We cried. The local paper wrote a great article about how many lives Dana had touched. The U.S. Postal Service even did a big story about her in their newsletter to postal workers nationwide.

One year later Dana surprised us. She arranged an even bigger surprise parade to celebrate us. There were huge signs. She presented us with a key to the city. We're still trying to find a way to thank her. Maybe one day we'll be able to surprise her again with something even bigger. Maybe we'll write a book and include her in it?

#60 Throw a POP-UP ART SHOW

A few photos from the art show
Bailey and her friends threw with
the Edgehill community.

"The world would be more awesome if we made time to sit on porches with people we may not know that well."

We ask most of our contributors to complete the sentence, "The world would be more awesome if _____." In Bailey Hazouri's case, she's living out the answer. Bailey, a college student from Tennessee, realized that she lived a very short distance from a housing community in the Edgehill district of Nashville and that she wanted to make a difference there. After giving some neighborhood siblings a ride to the hospital (their mom was giving birth!), Bailey was officially welcomed into the community by an invitation to play soccer on the following Saturday. Since then, she and her friends make it a point to play every Saturday. Bailey often hangs out on weekdays, too. "After a long day of work I'll sit on the porch with the kids' moms and talk while the kids play and do homework."

Bailey and her friends try to make each Saturday special. The events have ranged from back-to-school cookouts that include backpack giveaways to giant block parties with slip 'n' slides, to karaoke, to bouncy houses. It's all motivated by a sense of fun, of community—of just wanting to hang out with kids and be good neighbors. "There are a lot of shared meals and a lot of listening," Bailey says.

When Kid President and his team heard about Bailey, they wanted to help by throwing a Pop-Up Art Show. Bailey says, "The photo pop-up art show was an art show done by our kids. Kid President gave them each a disposable camera and asked them to take pictures of things they thought were beautiful, represented their neighborhood, or that they just liked. They took pictures of their parents, their siblings, their houses, their friends; some were of nature or of toys, or the park we played in. They were then developed in black and white and were hung from a pavilion in a nearby park. All the kids dressed up fancy and brought their parents. Getting to see the kids' faces as they ran around trying to find the ones they took, or seeing pictures of themselves was beautiful! I was so surprised and proud of how talented they were. I have never seen them be proud of something, and it was exciting to see them take joy in creating art."

Bailey and her friends are excited about being deeply, continually involved in the Edgehill community's life. "The kids keep coming back," Bailey says. "They introduce me to their moms, and write stories about Saturdays for their teachers at school. I got the privilege of going to kindergarten graduation and a few of our kids teachers came up to me and said how glad they were to meet 'Ms. Bailey.' I have never been so honored or humbled. I often ask myself after hard days if they even would notice if we never came back, but the truth is I think they would and that makes me smile."

"People need people," she says. "I am not a gifted speaker but God allows me to speak about Edgehill and my love for that neighborhood boldly. I'm thankful that people are interested in what goes on in our little park on Saturday afternoons."

BAILEY HAZOURI
Tennessee, USA

Why She's Awesome:
- She has a heart for kids and communities.
- She spends her free time as a college student trying to bridge divides.

TAKE SOMEONE'S PHOTO AND HAND-DELIVER IT TO THEM

JEREMY COWART is a famous celebrity photographer. But his real passion is taking photos of people in need—people like the homeless, orphans, the elderly, army vets, and single parents—and delivering the images to them.

Does taking lots of selfies and posting them online make you a photographer?
No, I think that makes you a selfieographer. Or a selfographer? A photographer is typically someone who points the camera at other people or things, not themselves.

What's it like to photograph famous people?
There are always lots of challenges with photographing famous people. But at the end of the day, they're just like you and me. They don't love having their pictures taken, but luckily for them, they have lots of people to make their hair, makeup, and clothes look absolutely perfect. Then someone gets on a computer and makes them look even MORE perfect. Fun for them, but not really fair to the rest of us.

People are just people, right?
Absolutely! Everyone just wants to love and be loved.

What made you want to be a photographer?
Being a photographer is kind of like having a birthday every day. You never know what surprise is next. You never know where you're traveling next, or who you're going to meet next. It is always an adventure!

When did you realize you could use photography to make the world more awesome?
After my first trip to Africa, I realized that photography could really help tell people's stories, or help a good organization, or help raise money to build a well. Organizations need to tell a good story and to tell a good story, they need good photos.

What is Help-Portrait?
Help-Portrait is a movement of photographers all over the world helping people in need by taking their pictures.

How does it work?
Easy. Find someone in need. Take their picture. Print their picture. And deliver it.

Opposite

"I met this woman in Seattle a few years ago. She had just lost her husband a couple weeks before this photo was taken. She said that while he was alive, they had never taken a photo as a family. So she gave me a photo of her deceased husband and asked if I could take her photo with their children and combine them with her husband's photo in Photoshop. This photo shows the results. There were tears everywhere! This is what Help-Portrait is all about."

What are some of your favorite stories that have come out of Help-Portrait?
We've seen people get their first jobs by having their first headshots. We've had people mail their photos to family they haven't seen in decades. We've seen Help-Portrait events bring families together. We've seen 70-year-old women get their hair and makeup done for the first time EVER. We've seen photo industry competitors shoot together and become community. The stories are endless!

Why are photos important?
Photos are like celebration bookmarks . . . they mark the highlights of our lives.

What is one photo that is extra special to you?
Oh, this list is endless. But one that comes to mind is a photo my brother took of me throwing my daughter in the air last year at a Daddy/ Daughter dance. My brother sadly passed away, unexpectedly, a couple weeks later and that was the last photo he ever took of me.

What advice would you give to someone who wants to use something they love to make the world a better place?
Make sure it's actually something you love. If you love it, work hard and pour yourself into it. That becomes contagious to the world around you, and people will want to join your team.

What advice would you give to your 10-year-old self?
Stop being so quiet! I was a shy little guy. Kids are awesome and they need to believe that.

Finish this sentence: The world would be more awesome if _____ .
We'd all stop arguing and respect each other more! Less words, more love.

JEREMY COWART
Tennessee, USA

Why He's Awesome:
- His iPhone app OKDOTHIS helps others use their voice, ideas, and creativity.
- He recently adopted two children from Haiti.
- Two-man sand volleyball and sweet tea are two of his favorite things in the world.

#62
Give the World a

Reason to Dance.

(It's everybody's duty to do that.)

#63 Put tape on your nose. It's a great conversation starter.

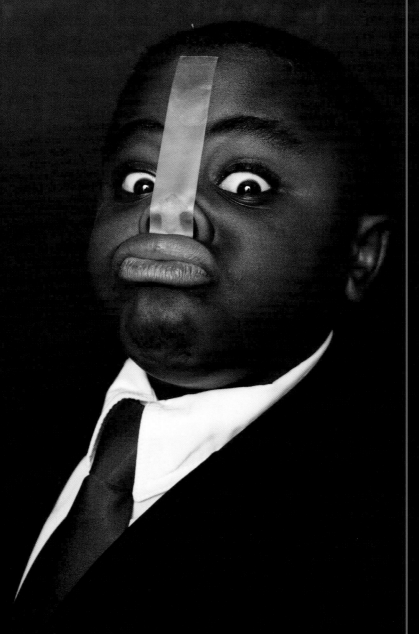

#64
COME UP WITH NAMES
FOR THINGS THAT ALREADY HAVE NAMES

Pants =
leg tubes

Dogs =
not cats

Cars =
land
boats

#65 MEOW THE

WORDS TO YOUR

FAVORITE SONGS

We call this cat caroling.

When Kid President looked for a partner to cat carol with him, he needed someone with a melodic voice, who could harmonize, and who wouldn't mind wearing a knit hat with cat ears. **CRAIG ROBINSON** was a perfect fit. Plus, he was super fun to hang out with. We asked Robinson about his experience cat caroling with KP.

What was your reaction when I told you we'd be going cat caroling?
My reaction to going cat caroling was . . . let's do it!!

Some of the people really made me laugh. What were your favorite reactions from people?
My favorite reaction was the guy who wanted us to stop as soon as we started. I believe you referred to him as a "tough crowd."

Why do you think music makes things better?
I think music makes things better because it touches the soul, it inspires, it evokes emotion, and it connects people.

It feels good to make people's day a little brighter. What's something someone's done that totally turned your day around?
One time, my friend took me from an okay day to a magically wonderful day . . . by taking me cat caroling.

What were you like when you were a kid?
When I was a kid, I was very shy and obedient and trusting. I always saw the good in people. Still do.

Do you have any embarrassing stories from when you were a kid?
One time when I was a kid, I was walking around naked in our house. I never walked around naked. I was sneaking so no one could see me, and I got a piece of cake out of the kitchen. As I was walking back upstairs, I didn't realize my parents had company, and I looked up and froze . . . looked them in the eye . . . naked . . . with cake in my mouth. I ran upstairs after that. Kept my clothes on after that, too.

What advice would you give to any kids reading this book?
The advice I would give to any kids reading this book is to love yourself, and be kind to others. You'll go far in life just by being kind.

Did you have fun surprising people with me?
I had a ball surprising people with you. The best part was how nicely they received us!

Besides cat caroling, what are some other ways we could help people have the best day of their lives so far?
We could have disco dancing parties and sing-alongs! We could also pass out cupcakes—that would turn anybody's day around.

Finish this sentence: The world would be more awesome if _____.
Everyone treated each other with love, kindness, and respect.

Would you go cat caroling with me again sometime?
Say the word, and I'm there.

#66 BEHOLD the POWER of ⦂POSITIVE PARTYING⦂

ANDREW W.K. is the world's No. 1 party expert. We asked him about the possibility of being a 24/7 party person.

Thanks for being in my book. High five! Why do you think high fives ever caught on in the first place?
Thank you for having me in your book! I think high fives caught on because they rule. There's no other explanation. They feel great, especially when you really smack hard and get a good sting. If they weren't awesome, then people wouldn't do them.

I need your help. Define the word "party."
To party is to do what you like, and to like what you do. You live every day as a party. How? Just by partying. Every day. All day. And night, too. A lot of people told me it was impossible to party nonstop all the time forever. But so far, I've been able to do it. Thanks to you and a lot of other people, too. It's a group effort. I couldn't do it alone. Partying is a team sport.

What made you want to become a party?
Well, I wanted to get cheered up, so I thought of the most fun thing I could think of, which was the word "PARTY," and then I just decided to just make that my life.

How can you make every day a party for the people around you?
The partiest people are the ones who don't tell other people how to party. Just do what you love and the rest will take care of itself. Do what you were born to do, and let the people around you do what they feel they were born to do. Never try and force someone to party. That isn't very party at all. It's way partier to let everyone have fun however they want and just be nice.

Life is tough sometimes. How do you stay so enthusiastic about life?
Just by partying as much as I can. The more we're faced with challenging times, the more this party power really comes in handy. On a good day, we party. On a bad day, we party until it becomes a good day. If you think about a problem in a bunch of different ways, eventually you'll find a way that makes it a party. And then you might realize it wasn't even a problem to begin with. It was just a different kind of party.

What advice would you give to your 10-year-old self?
That you really can become a professional partier, so don't listen to anyone who says otherwise.

What if you don't feel like partying?
Then I just party some more, and the feeling of not wanting to party goes away. It's possible to party even while you're not partying. It just takes more effort.

Finish this sentence: The world would be more awesome if _____.
Everyone realized how awesome the world already is. And had a party about it.

#67

SPREAD CONFETTI

(THE EARTH-FRIENDLY

KIND)!

There are so many moments in life that would be better with confetti. At just the perfect moment, the music hits, and the confetti drops, and everybody celebrates! Awesome, right? Just one problem: It can make a mess and be dangerous to birds, small children, and curious people who like to eat things they find on the ground.

Some solutions to this problem:

1. Create your own confetti out of biodegradable and water-soluble paper!
2. Who said confetti has to be paper? Just arrange for water to rain down on everyone. It is eco-friendly and water-soluble because it is water.
3. If you can't create confetti, at least create confetti-worthy moments for the people around you.

(#68) Be kind.
It's not always easy, but it's always important.

In moments when you've had a good night's sleep, a great meal, and life is peachy, kindness can come easy.

In moments where somebody you barely know says something hurtful about your mom or your face or your mom's face, kindness can be difficult.

In moments like this, you're gonna want to be not awesome for a bit. That's understandable. You're a person.

Pause. Remember they're a person, too.

If you want to make a difference, you have to be different. We've got a whole world to make awesome. There's no time to be mean. You're in the business of treating everybody like they're a somebody, so save your energy. It won't always be easy, but it will always be worth it.

MOMENTS WHEN IT'S NOT EASY TO BE KIND

WHEN YOU DROP YOUR ICE CREAM CONE.

SOMEBODY SAYS SOMETHING NOT AWESOME ABOUT YOUR DROPPED ICE CREAM CONE.

IT'S ME! YOUR ICE CREAM CONE! WHY'D YOU DROP ME? WHY? WHY?

SOMEBODY CALLS YOU IN THE MIDDLE OF THE NIGHT PRETENDING TO BE YOUR ICE CREAM CONE.

NOT COOL.

#69 WRITE A POEM
for somebody who doesn't normally get poems written about them

Throughout history, people have written grand, epic poems about warriors and adventurers to ensure that their tales get passed down for generations to come. Show somebody you think their greatness deserves to be recognized in the same way. Take time to write an epic poem about the adventures of your garbage man, your favorite librarian, or your mom.

#70 Gather your friends, dress up like SUPERHEROES, and do someone's yard work

#71 WEAR SOMETHING AWESOME

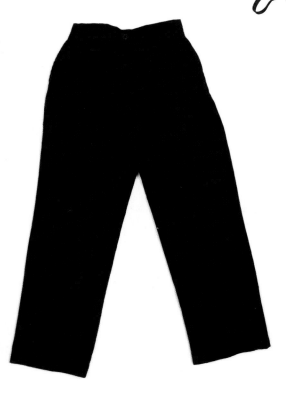

Classic white button-up dress shirt. Stains from meals add character.

Simple two-button jacket in a polyester blend. Usually unbuttoned to allow room for dancing.

Robby's tie is always perfectly tied because it's a zipper tie.

Elegant black socks. Just kidding. They're just socks that are black.

Solid black high-top Chuck Taylors. They look a lot cooler than they smell.

Elastic waistband for comfort (and dancing.)

MEET MOZIAH

MOZIAH BRIDGES loves bow ties. Here, he talks about his "passion for fashion" and about his company, Mo's Bows.

Mo! How'd you get so stylish?
I'm stylish because of my dad and granddad. Both of them are musicians and always knew fashion and style. They wore suits for no reason at all, so when my mom let me dress myself I wore suits for no special reason. She never made me change because that's what I wanted to wear.

As Kid President, I'm a big suit-and-tie guy. What is it that you love about bow ties?
I love bow ties because they make you look good and feel good, and when you wear a bow tie you just stand out from other guys wearing a necktie. I always tell my customers that "guys who wear neckties have to; but guys who wear bow ties want to."

What made you want to start making and selling your own bow ties?
I started making them because I wanted to wear them, but I started selling them because other people wanted to wear them. I gave away a lot of free bow ties but everyone just kept asking, so I decided to sell them so I could buy fabric to make more.

So now you have your own business? How's that working out?
It's working out great. It's fun because I'm really trying to set a fashion trend for our generation.

What advice would you give to any kids out there who might want to start their own business?
To figure out what you like doing and find out how to make money doing it. I liked to dress in suits and ties so I turned it into a business. My passion is fashion.

Any advice for people who might not feel like they have style?
Everyone has their own type of style so to me there is no such thing as "no style." Style is in the person.

What's the secret to dressing awesome?
The BIG secret is so simple: You just have to wear what speaks to YOU. And know that you are awesome in whatever you wear.

How can dressing awesome help make the world more awesome?
When people dress with confidence they will feel awesome and then BAZAAM! The world would be more awesome.

Finish this sentence: The world would be more awesome if _____ .
Everyone could rock a Mo's Bow.

MOZIAH BRIDGES
Tennessee, USA

Why He's Awesome:
- He started a business at the age of 9.
- He's fashion forward.
- He wears suits and bow ties "just because."

#72 INVENT A DANCE

THE PENCIL SHARPENER

Do the Grocery Store Shuffle. Start an Elevator Joy Bomb. Or, honor someone you love by naming the dance after them.

Typically, dances are named by describing the moves within them, but you're more awesome than that. Not only do you invent new dances constantly (see above), but you name them after people you think deserve their own dance.

This dance is called "The Pencil Sharpener."

#73 JOIN A MOVEMENT!

Being awesome and helping people isn't about getting people to notice you. Sometimes you need to do something to help somebody, and there's no need for them to know you did it. Do it anyway.

Some of the best and most important things you'll ever do will never be seen by people. Do them anyway. At first, it might be hard to not get credit for something you put a lot of time and effort into, but you'll find it's more rewarding to do something just because it's the right thing to do, not because you want the applause.

CHAPTER 7

#74 MAKE SOMETHING AWESOME!

You don't need a lot of money. You don't need a lot of power. You just need to care.

You have everything you need to make the world a little more awesome.

The world is changed by ordinary people living out big love. It's one person so filled with love that they have to live it out. They do something awesome for somebody, and then that person is filled with love. It just goes on and on and on. Everything isn't awesome, but you are.

Some people might think it's impossible to change things. You can see how they could think that. We live in a world with kids who are hungry, people who are homeless, and worse. It's important to remember this: Things don't have to stay the way they are. The world is changed by ordinary people who decide to do something extraordinary. You're one of those people.

Get to it.

Above
Top
Kid President cupcake
by Michele McAtee,
(Maddiebird Bakery,
Illinois, USA).

Bottom
Fan art by Mikołaj Strug
(Lubelskie, Poland).

SEAL OF THE TINY PRESIDENT OF THE UNITED STATES

PRESIDENT

HERE'S WHAT WE USE:

1. old sheet of cardboard
2. hand-drawn presidential seal
3. blue curtains
4. broken record player (found on the side of the road)
5. old soup can
6. yarn
7. books to make the desk's height just right

#75 Start with your (HEART) and then JUST START

When **VIVIENNE HARR** saw a photo of two boys living in slavery, she knew she had to do something. So she created a lemonade stand to raise money to end childhood slavery. Did we mention she's only 10?

Can lemonade change the world?
Well, lemonade can't. But lemon-AID can! Hee hee! You also need an awesome "small group of thoughtful committed citizens," just like Margaret Mead said!

What is Make a Stand?
It's more than a product. It's a promise. It's about finding what is in your heart, turning your compassion into action, and never ever giving up. The world needs more people who do that.

Why a lemonade stand?
It was the only business experience I had. I went with what I knew—and it grew and grew and grew! Big things have small beginnings!

How much have you raised so far?
We've raised more than $100,000 to eradicate child slavery. And with our new mobile crowdfunding app, we hope to raise many more millions.

What have been your top 5 favorite moments along your journey?
#1. The first day of my stand, when I had no idea what would happen, but I knew we were facing in the right direction. It's important to face in the right direction!
#2. Singing "Firework" by Katy Perry in Times Square in 2012 when I reached my first $100,000 goal.
#3. Bottling our hope—and seeing our first bottles in stores!
#4. Ringing the bell for the Twitter IPO where I said, "Today we rang the bell for hope and freedom."
#5. Speaking at the United Nations on behalf of all enslaved children in the world.

What do you say to people who might think they can't make a difference?
You don't have to be big or powerful to change the world. You can be just like me! Start with your heart . . . and then just start.

Finish this sentence: The world would be more awesome if _____.
Everyone made a stand for what they believed in!

VIVIENNE HARR
California, USA

Why She's Awesome:
- Her Make a Stand story was made into a real-life movie; the documentary #standwithme released in 2014.
- She's spoken in front of the United Nations and at giant international events all about saving children.
- On her first day, she beat her dad's lemonade stand record.

#76   Be generous. GIVE!

Our friend **JEFF SHINABARGER** is a problem solver. He's always on the lookout for creative ways people can help solve problems in the world. Gift Card Giver is just one of many brilliant projects he's made happen, and it's a great way you can help by using something you probably have already.

What does Gift Card Giver do?

We collect unused or partially used gift cards and then give them to people and organizations in need. Every day we receive gift cards in the mail from people have generously donated their leftover balances to help those in need. We also receive applications from people who have a need that could be met with gift cards. We check the balances on all the gift cards that are sent to us, and then once we have a good amount to a certain store, we match the gift cards with the needs and ship them off!

That's cool. What is a cool story that has come out of this?

Julian is a young boy born prematurely who has had a life of medical complications as a result. He and his family now face having to travel far from home to receive the medical care he needs to be free from a tube in his neck that helps him breathe, but makes it difficult to eat. Kelly from the Granted Wish Foundation reached out to us to assist their efforts to help this family with their travel for Julian's care. We were able to send cards for gas, fast food, and even Toys "R" Us because of the donations we have received.

What advice would you give to your 10-year-old self?

Fear will always be part of life, but don't let fear hold you back from pursuing what only you can do. We are all made to do something unique, so push through fear and do it.

Who inspires you?

I am always inspired when people are pursuing something that is impossible with new ideas that have not been considered before. I love seeing young people striving to make things better in a broken world. Creativity unique to others stories is always a beautiful sight that I want to see more of.

Finish this sentence: The world would be more awesome if _____.

Every office had a Slurpee machine and more people gave their lives to solving problems in their communities.

I have a gift card in my pocket right here. What do I do?

Well, you can either keep it or you can give it to Gift Card Giver! If you choose to meet needs with it, you can check the balance on it, write it on the card with a Sharpie, and then you can send it to: PO Box 17920, Atlanta, GA 30316.

JEFF SHINABARGER
Georgia, USA

Why He's Awesome:

- He and his wife created Gift Card Giver, an organization that gives gift cards to people and organizations in need.
- He is the founder of Plywood People, a community for problem-solving and collaboration.

#77 USE YOUR IMAGINATION!

It's easy to make fun of stuff, but it's cooler to make stuff. A couple of years ago, a 9-year-old boy named Caine reminded us about this with his elaborate cardboard arcade. His imagination and creativity inspired our friend, filmmaker **NIRVAN MULLICK**, *to make the short film* Caine's Arcade. *More than 9 million people saw Caine's story and joined the movement to encourage kids to dream and play. Nirvan told us about his journey.*

One day, I went to buy a door handle for my car. I have an old car, and I had put off fixing it all summer. I pulled into a random used auto parts store in an industrial part of East Los Angeles. And when I walked inside, I met a 9-year-old boy named Caine, the owner's son, who was standing behind an elaborate arcade he had built using cardboard boxes out of old auto parts containers. During his summer vacation, he had gone to work with his dad and started building this arcade, and gradually he had taken over the entire front half of the auto shop. It looked amazing.

Caine asked me if I wanted to play, so I asked him how it worked. He told me that for $1, I could get 4 turns, or for $2 I could get a "Fun Pass" that was good for 500 turns. The Fun Pass seemed like an awesome deal, so I gave him $2. Caine rang me up on his cardboard cash register, stamped my hand, and gave me my Fun Pass; I then spent the next 40 minutes playing Caine's cardboard games. They were so much fun! My favorite game was the soccer game, where you had to flick a paper ball into a goal blocked by toy army soldiers. When I scored a goal, Caine would crawl inside the box and push out prize tickets, just like at a real arcade. He was even wearing a shirt that said "Caine's Arcade" on the back and "STAFF" on the front.

I was really inspired by Caine's creativity. Playing his arcade brought me back to my own childhood. When I was a kid, I liked to make stick forts and sand tunnels. I used to draw elaborate Rube Goldberg–like mousetraps, and carve miniature baseball bats out of sticks.

I decided to try to make a short film to share that feeling with more people. So I asked Caine's dad, George, if I could film his son's arcade. George said yes and told me that I had been Caine's first and only customer. All summer he had asked customers if they wanted to play, but no one had stopped to buy a Fun Pass.

This broke my heart, so as part of the film, we hatched a plan to try and make Caine's day by organizing a surprise flashmob of customers to come play Caine's Arcade. I posted an invitation online, and the flashmob took off. On the day of the surprise, Caine's dad took him to get pizza, while hundreds of people showed up. When they came back from lunch, there were more than 100 people waiting for him at his arcade, cheering, "We came to play!"

Caine's face lit up with a huge smile. Then he got right to work! People played Caine's games late into the night. On his way home, Caine told his dad that this was the best day of his whole life.

The response after I posted the video online was beyond anything I had imagined. I set up a scholarship for Caine with the hope of raising $25,000 for Caine's college education, but the first day the film posted, it got more than 1 million views, and we raised $60,000 for Caine. To date, the video has more than 9 million views and has raised more than $239,000 for Caine's Scholarship Fund.

Caine's Arcade trended on Twitter, there were news stories everywhere, and tens of thousands of people started to come play Caine's Arcade from all around the world! The first weekend, there was a four-hour line of people waiting to play.

The most amazing response for me, however, was from kids. Kids who saw the film were inspired to start making their own cardboard arcade games. Parents started sharing photos on our Facebook page of the awesome things kids were making inspired by the film.

I realized that there were kids like Caine in every neighborhood and in every community around the world. I started to think that maybe there was a way to help foster their creativity as well. So I started a non-profit called the Imagination Foundation with the Goldhirsh Foundation. Our goal is to foster creativity and entrepreneurship in kids worldwide. About six months in, we announced our first Global Cardboard Challenge, where kids around the world build awesome things using cardboard and recycled materials culminating in a global "Day of Play." This will be our third year in a row now, and more than 100,000 kids in 50 countries will take part.

Imagination is what allows us to dream up new things. There are a lot of big challenges in the world, and things are changing faster than ever, so we need a new generation of creative problem solvers. We need kids who can build the world they imagine, and also imagine the world we can build. They just need the confidence to know we believe in them.

Caine and I get invited around the world to share our story. Along the way, Caine gained a lot of creative confidence. His dad told me that Caine's grades had improved, and that he even stopped stuttering.

I don't think play is something you ever really out grow. We all start out creative, but often it gets forgotten or even unlearned as we grow up. I truly believe that if more people played, the world would be a happier place. We would have more swing sets and four square and less stress and heart attacks.

My hope is that if we raise a generation of creative problem solvers, we will be able to solve our most challenging problems, from climate change to extreme poverty to war. And what keeps me going is the opportunity to make someone's day through expressing my own creativity. You can do something small for one person, and it can change the world.

NIRVAN MULLICK
California, USA

Why He's Awesome:
Caine's Arcade and the Imagination Foundation (@imagination) help kids everywhere be creative.
He reminds grown-ups and parents and teachers that play is important for learning.
He was brave enough to remind us all: Never pass up an opportunity to buy a Fun Pass.

#78 SPEND TIME WITH YOUR FAMILY!

It's not easy to be in sync, even when you're with family . . . sometimes especially when you're with family. If you're **LENNON** and **MAISY STELLA**, though, being in sync comes pretty naturally. Maybe that's because they come from a musical family. We asked the *Nashville* stars about the good and the bad of creating music with your family.

You come from a musical family. What does everyone play?
Maisy: Well, my sister, Lennon, she plays guitar, ukulele, and piano. I play the same instruments as her. We also both play the drums—just for fun. But my dad basically plays every instrument, like, literally known to man (laughs). He can pick up anything and know how to play it, just automatically. My mom plays guitar, ukulele, and piano.

What's it like making music with your family?
Lennon: It's awesome. It is a really cool experience. You know, making music on your own is wicked, but then making it with your family and people you love and choose to spend time with is just awesome.

How have your parents inspired and encouraged you to create music?
Lennon: You know, it's like I grew up—Maisy, too—we both grew up completely engulfed in music.
Maisy: When they played music, we played music. When they sang, we sang. It was just always that way.
Lennon: I have always been inspired by that and have always wanted to write and to play music in every way, in every aspect because of them. So I think they're definitely the main reason me and Maisy are interested in it at all.

How do you make each other better performers and better people?
Maisy: She influences me on everything. She influences what I listen to. She will be playing a song in the car that I have never heard before and I will instantly fall in love with it. And we have a phone connection, which is amazing (laughs), so when she buys a song, I will get the song, so it is perfect because all of my favorite songs of hers come to my phone.
Lennon: We just complement each other. We reflect off of each other's emotions. And as a performer, I learn from Maisy all the time.

What are the challenges and benefits of working with family?
Maisy: There are benefits, of course, because I get to do it with the person I love the most. So there's nothing bad about it.
Lennon: In the end, we are family and we love each other. I mean, we spend so much time together. We are bound to have some sort of bump in the road, but I feel like when we do have little arguments, we always know it will come back to loving each other and wanting to be able to sing together, so we just kind of have to get over it, I guess (laughs).

What advice would you want to give to families?
Maisy: Try not to fight because it is not fun being onstage with somebody that you are not happy with. (laughs)
Lennon: Love one another. Don't take each other for granted because it is easy to forget how much work everyone is putting into things. Just be constantly loving and just don't take advantage of it.

BROADCAST THE GOOD NEWS AROUND YOU

Create your own news show for your school or workplace. Develop a newsletter. Write a blog post. Do whatever it takes to make sure good news spreads faster than bad news.

#80 START SIMPLE

At school, **CASSANDRA LIN** joined a group project that quickly turned into something more. She and her classmate John Perino found a way to do something that would change the lives of people in their community. Their community service team created a sustainable system for collecting waste cooking oil and converting it into bio-fuel. This fuel is then distributed to local families in need of heating assistance. It's called Project: Turn Grease Into Fuel or Project TGIF for short, and we think it's awesome.

What sort of response did you get when you shared the idea?
We began TGIF during the 5th grade. When we found out that waste could be turned into fuel, it seemed logical for us to bring both the community and environment together to create one solution! At first, people were skeptical that a group of 5th-graders wanted to create such an ambitious project. But after we set up our first public grease receptacle and donated the first check for heating oil, the whole community was rooting for us!

How does it work?
Project TGIF is a sustainable system that collects waste cooking oil from residents and businesses and converts it into biodiesel fuel. To date, TGIF has distributed 29,000 gallons of biofuel to help heat the homes of 290 families. The TGIF program currently helps about 80 families every year.

What does it feel like to be part of providing solutions to people in need?
It's so surreal to think of the impact the project has on the community just by providing something as simple as heating oil. So many people overlook this as a basic need, and it fills us all with pride knowing that we can alleviate such a burden from a family struggling financially.

People all over the world have been inspired by what you're doing! Why do you think it has connected with so many people?
I think this project has connected with so many people because it seems like such a simple idea and it makes people think, "Why aren't we doing this in our community?" Social media has been great at spreading the word about our project, and we hope that people will be inspired to take action after hearing about our work!

Finish this sentence: The world would be more awesome if_____.
We all made an effort to treat each other better. Being thoughtful and kind towards others can go a long way.

CASSANDRA LIN
Rhode Island, USA

Why She's Awesome:
- She created Project TGIF (Turn Grease Into Fuel).
- She worked and collaborated with her family to create her project.
- She's working to help stop global warming.

CASSANDRA LIN

#81 Do WHAT YOU LIKE, and share it with others

RAY TOLLISON and his sons, Sam and Ben, both 10 at the time, realized that a lot of refugee kids in the United States had no toys, so they decided to make monsters for them. We love this idea, and we love monsters, so we asked them to tell us about A Monster to Love.

What exactly is A Monster to Love?
At A Monster to Love, we create monsters from the finest fabrics in the land, stuffed to cuddly perfection. When you buy a monster, we give a monster to a child who could really use a monster to love.

How did this come about?
Our super duper friend Lindsey was going to visit some refugee kids who, along with their families, had just been resettled in the United States. They were in the hospital and after talking to the boys about refugees we decided to make some monsters for them. After making the monsters, we took a quick photo and posted it on Facebook, and A Monster to Love began! It has been 3 years, and we have given away more than 2,000 monsters.

So who does what?
Ben is the Chief Monster Drawer/Designer. Sam is the Chief Monster Maker/Sewer, and Ray is the Dad/Driver/Scheduler/Sewer and filler inner wherever needed.

What's it like working on this together as a family?
It is fun working and traveling together, but we do not always agree. In those cases we have to put things to a vote, flip a coin, or participate in a quick round of Rock, Paper, Scissors to work it out. Teamwork is the key around Monster HQ. We really collaborate on everything and this makes all of our toys better.

How can kids and grown-ups dream up something of their own to help people all over the world?
Do what you like and share it with others. To all of you adults out there: Work with a kid or maybe a couple of kids! You will be amazed at the ideas that they have, and you just may have a ton of fun helping them build something awesome.

Finish this sentence: The world would be more awesome if _____.
Everybody had a monster to love! —Sam
Donuts randomly fell out of the sky. —Ben
We put glitter and sparkles on everything. —Zoie (a.k.a. monster sister)

SAM & BEN TOLLISON
Colorado, USA

Why They're Awesome:
- A family project with a dad and his two sons—what's not to love!
- They were inspired to help after learning about a local problem.
- They make soft and squishy monsters that don't scare kids but help kids. Did we mention they're soft?

#82
Give
Out
handmade
Awards

Take time to celebrate people you think are making things better where you live. You could host an awards show or simply deliver the award directly to them wherever they are.

We created a simple little handmade award to present to people making our neighborhood a better place. We call it a "Neighborhoodie." It's just a very small baby hoodie spray painted gold, covered in glitter, and attached to a block of wood, but it's the thought that counts. Right? And here's the thought: Sometimes little things could be a big deal to somebody who needs encouragement. You can call your award whatever. It doesn't have to be a tiny hoodie spray painted gold. Think of somebody you think deserves an award. Create it. Give it to them. It's that easy.

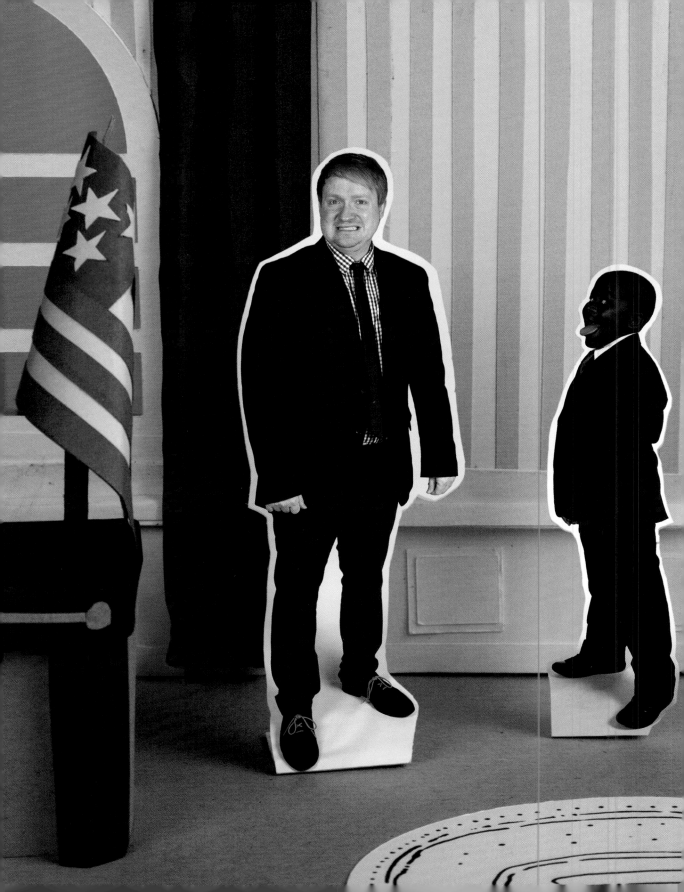

CHAPTER 8:

LICK THE

Walls of the

WHITE HOUSE

#83 LICK THE Walls of the WHITE HOUSE

I really feel like this should say, "Don't lick the walls of the White House."

Aw! I like it as it is!

I know, but it implies that people should actively pursue licking the walls of the White House.

Well, I did it!

Yes, and the Secret Service asked you to stop.

You win.

Opposite
Robby hides in the bushes
on the front lawn of the
White House.

Above Left
Brad and Robby in front
of the U.S. Capitol in
Washington, DC.

Above Right
Robby in front of the White
House South Portico during
rehearsal for the Easter
Egg Roll.

There are some moments that happen in life when words simply fail. Hearing a Secret Service agent say, "Um . . . sir . . . please don't lick the walls of the White House" is just one of those moments.

In 2013 we were invited to attend the 135th annual White House Easter Egg Roll, an event that goes all the way back to 1878, when President Rutherford B. Hayes invited kids to play on the White House lawn for the day. When we received the phone call, we attempted to act cool, as though we got phone calls like that all the time, but after hanging up, there was a lot of screaming and dancing and more screaming.

We loaded up our entire family and made our way to Washington, DC. Driving past all the beautiful monuments, historic landmarks, and important government buildings, we were awestruck. We were also full of questions: How is it that our journey could have led us here? Did they mean to invite someone else? Didn't they realize we were just ordinary people from a town about the size of the White House lawn?

And, of course, the biggest question of all: Would we get to meet the actual president of the United States?

ROBBY & BO →

Two White House staffers greeted us kindly upon our arrival. They helped lead us through security, down winding paths, and, eventually, to the actual steps of the actual White House. Surprisingly, we would immediately meet one of our first Obamas: Bo.

Robby immediately hit it off with the First Family's dog, declaring him to be the softest dog he had ever met.

> He felt like a cloud.

> A cloud?

> Yes, he felt like a little dog cloud. I love him. I miss him.

> Maybe someone will read this book to him, and he'll hear your message.

> A boy can dream. I love you, Bo!

Each year, to kick off the large-scale event, the president and his family address the more than 30,000 people gathered on the lawn from the White House balcony. It's a grand moment leading into what annually becomes a playful, lighthearted day when the country is given a reminder that the White House really is the "People's House."

This year we were told that Robby would be the one introducing the Obama family.

We again attempted to act like this was normal. Our eyes large, we looked at each other and made "What in the world is happening right now?" faces. We were screaming on the inside but agreed that we both had to hold together our excitement and act cool. This was a big deal. We had to act respectable. We couldn't let the bigness get to us.

It got to us.

We were guided through several beautiful rooms of the White House. Each room seemed grander than the one before. You could see and smell and feel the weight of history everywhere. They led us to a small waiting area directly beside the balcony where Robby would address more than 30,000 people. This would be the same balcony where we would meet our country's president and his family. We should have been excited, but we were nervous.

They seated us in two old wooden chairs against a wall. This would be our temporary home as we waited for the event to begin. We were left alone with our nerves for what seemed like an eternity. As a distraction, we focused on different things (Brad on a large painting of President Abraham Lincoln; Robby stood in his chair). I was biting my fingernails. Robby was rubbing the walls. We were not ourselves.

Why are you rubbing the wallpaper?

It's soft.

That doesn't mean you have to touch it! Act like you are in the White House.

I was biting my fingernails. Robby was rubbing the walls. We were not ourselves.

Opposite
Robby with the
First Dog Bo.

Right
Robby showing off on the
president's basketball court.

Then it happened. A Secret Service agent entered the room. At this point, Robby was standing in his chair and had decided to see what the wallpaper felt like on his face. Robby paused with his face pressed against the wall. The Secret Service agent shuffled his eyebrows.

His delivery was slow and deliberate. He said with a slight grin, "Um . . . sir . . . please don't lick the walls of the White House."

It was clear this was a sentence he had never had to say before.

Robby quickly moved back to his seat. We both turned completely red and sat in stunned silence. Neither of us said anything until a short moment later when we realized what had just happened. Suddenly we had a new problem: We couldn't stop laughing.

Below
Robby and Brad take a selfie before the White House Easter Egg Roll.

Opposite
Robby on the balcony of the White House.

> You didn't actually lick the White House, though, did you?

> I did.

> Why? I thought the Secret Service guy just thought you were going to lick the wall.

> I was nervous!

> I know of absolutely no one else who does that when they're nervous.

> Well, I do! I wanted to see what it tasted like. It tasted like silk.

> Silk? That's not a taste. . . .

> Ha-ha-ha-ha.

> Oh, man. Well, it was a strange moment that I will definitely remember forever.

> Yes, it was. Also it was embarrassing.

> Now you admit it. There we go.

In life you'll end up in lots of places you never imagined. Don't let your nerves overtake you so much that you can't enjoy it. You might end up getting so confused that you find yourself licking the walls. Don't lick the walls. And if you do, try to laugh about it.

#84
TAKE A MOMENT TO REFLECT

What was it like to be on that balcony with the president and everyone?

The view was awesome.

Your mom and dad said they could only see the top of your head from below.

Yeah! The balcony rail was right at my head. That was bad. It helped keep me from being too nervous, though.

What was it like meeting the First Family?

The First Family?

Yeah, that's what they call the president and his family.

Oh. Good.

Seriously? That's it? Good.

You know what I mean. I loved it! They were really nice and made me feel like I was at home.

You felt like you were at home?

Well, I wasn't gonna get food out of their fridge or anything like that.

No, I know, but you liked the White House?

I did. A lot.

Would you want to live there one day and be the real president?

No way. Too much paperwork.

Our trip to the White House wasn't even halfway over, and we had already acquired a mountain of memories. It had been a magical morning full of stories we continue to recall fondly. Sure, there was that whole thing with licking the walls of the White House just before going out on the balcony. But that was all behind us. We were prepared to go home from Washington, DC, happy and satisfied that we had met the First Family and that Robby's introduction of them had gone great. Then came a tap on the shoulder from one of the friendly White House staff friends who had been with us throughout the day.

"The president would like to see you in 15 minutes," he said. We thought he was kidding. He wasn't kidding.

We were whisked away from the lawn and led to the West Wing. We entered through a secure door and then through another. There were large photo prints all over the walls of great men and women who had been through these halls to meet with the president. Dignitaries, leaders, movers and shakers from all over the world. We were two ordinary people from a small town in Tennessee who made some silly videos on the internet. Should we tell them

there had been a mistake before it was too late?

President Obama was standing just outside the entryway to his office. He smiled and welcomed us in. What followed was a tour of the Oval Office and a conversation we'll never forget. Not only were we standing in the president's office, but we had been invited in. Robby was even invited to sit behind the commander in chief's desk.

Below
President Obama welcomes Kid President into the Oval Office.

Opposite
Robby makes himself at home behind the president's desk.

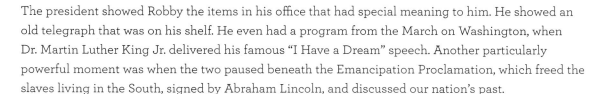

What was it like to sit behind the real president's desk?

It was awesome! It's really big.

I was concerned that you immediately wanted to pick up the president's phone. The president looked concerned, too.

I just wanted to say hi to all the troops.

That's not how it works.

Yeah, I just wanted to say, "Hey guys! It's me. Keep doing it." Or something like that.

I think the president reached to grab the phone from you and said something like, "Okay. Let's be careful not to start an international incident."

I would've just said, "Hello."

That would've been a nice thought, but I think it's good he stopped you.

The president showed Robby the items in his office that had special meaning to him. He showed an old telegraph that was on his shelf. He even had a program from the March on Washington, when Dr. Martin Luther King Jr. delivered his famous "I Have a Dream" speech. Another particularly powerful moment was when the two paused beneath the Emancipation Proclamation, which freed the slaves living in the South, signed by Abraham Lincoln, and discussed our nation's past.

We had been a little disappointed when our time with the president earlier in the day had been so rushed. There had been no time for anything beyond small talk. Now we somehow found ourselves

"The most important thing we can all do is treat each other with kindness and respect."

President Obama

inside the Oval Office. This was an impromptu visit, so we weren't prepared for an interview. We did, however, come to Washington, DC, prepared with at least one question for the president, just in case the opportunity presented itself. Now was the perfect time.

Robby pulled out a small note card from his suit jacket pocket. He then asked the question we had prepared: "How can kids and grown-ups work together to change the world?"

The president's response was immediate, thoughtful, and spot on:

"The most important thing we can all do is treat each other with kindness and respect. Kids, they can learn right away, in school and the playground, to be nice to each other. . . . You treat everybody fairly, no matter what they look like or where they're from and if you start learning to do that as kids, and everybody is respectful and nice to each other, then when they grow up, they'll be doing the same thing and we'll have a lot fewer problems."

We then sat with the president and discussed with him our dreams for kids. He presented Robby with a presidential yo-yo (among other gifts, but this is the one that received the most enthusiasm from Robby).

because we were still in disbelief that it had even happened. Our friends and fans cheered us on and shared the story.

Interestingly, several blogs and commentators criticized the president for taking time to talk to a 9-year-old instead of doing something "more important." But MSNBC's Lawrence O'Donnell didn't agree. He said:

"It's funny, it's cute, it's truly awesome. And not just because Robby says it's awesome. Some people in our office today cried when they watched it, and couldn't say exactly why. And, I think it's because this man, and this little boy, together, tell us a story that is deeply profound, without ever trying to be profound. They just meet and chat and laugh. But they do it in the Oval Office.

"And their meeting in that room can't help but evoke our painful past and our always hopeful future. This meeting in the Oval Office is empty of politics and full of love and hope and grace. You can see in it more hope for this country's ideal than any speech could ever deliver. The ideal that any child in this country can grow up to be president.

"Yeah. We get to live in a country where that happened."

Opposite
President Obama explains the Emancipation Proclamation to Robby.

Above
Forgoing a handshake, the two presidents hug.

He said, "You keep doing the great work you're doing. Even though we're presidents, can we still hug?" They hugged and even closed out their time together with a high five.

We posted the video of Kid President with President Obama online a few days later. We were so happy to have a record of it

#85 KISS BEYONCÉ

Hey, this doesn't belong. This is a list of 100 Awesome Ideas to make the world a better place.

This is an awesome thing. I kissed Beyoncé.

Yes, but . . .

You are just jealous.

I just think . . .

I kissed Beyoncé, and it was awesome! Put it in.

"Hello, Beyoncé! My name is Kid President."
"Oh, I know that. You're my favorite."
"You're MY favorite!"
"No. You're MY favorite!"

About a year into making our videos, we created a video of Kid President playing with chicken nuggets. In the video, he held up two nuggets and designated one of them as himself and the other Beyoncé. He then began to detail what an interview between the two of them would be like. We sent this video to Beyoncé's team and they responded back: She loved it!

It was in this moment we learned the magic of chicken nuggets.

How can you use the magic of chicken nuggets to help make somebody's life a little more awesome? Maybe your parents' wedding video got erased. Reenact this great moment in your family's history with chicken nuggets! Maybe something really cool happened, and you thought it was captured with your camera, but it wasn't. Just grab some chicken nuggets and act it out. It's just like the real thing—except with chicken nuggets.

KID PRESIDENT: THE BEYONCÉ INTERVIEW

So Beyoncé . . . (starts laughing, then composes himself) who encouraged you when you were a kid?
My mother encouraged me. And I think it's so important at that age to feel safe and to know you have someone there supporting you and standing by you.

Do you like the video I made for you?
I absolutely love the video you made for me. I can't believe I'm sitting here with the Kid President. I was very excited to meet you today!

Why is World Humanitarian Day so important?
It's so admirable when people around the world dedicate their lives to other people. And it's so important for us to take some time and be unselfish and have compassion. Because we really can impact the world.

So, Beyoncé, what do you think the world needs more of?
Well, I think the world needs more strong, empowered men and women. So I say, the world needs more strength.

Ah, strength. Good answer. (pause) Are we best friends?
Only if I get a kiss on my cheek.

O . . . K . . .
C'mon, c'mon, c'mon, Kid President. (laughs and points at her cheek)

And then Kid President kissed Beyoncé. It's true. See page 190 for photographic evidence.

Thank you! (claps)

Thank you for doing this interview with me.

* This interview first appeared online at www.soulpancake.com/youtube as part of a project for World Humanitarian Day. Special thanks to the United Nations for making this possible.

#86
LET YOUR HEROES KNOW THEY ARE YOUR HEROES

Teachers matter. Outside of our families, teachers have the potential to shape us more than anyone else. But so often, great teachers are overlooked. What if we took the time to reward teachers for their service and reminded them how influential their guidance can be? With that question in mind, Kid President, SoulPancake, and Cole Elementary School set out to surprise a retiring 1st-grade teacher, Ms. Nancy Flexer, with a party full of her former students.

It was a typical school day. Outside of her classroom, Ms. Flexer, who would be retiring at the end of the school year, greeted her colleagues. "Good morning, everybody. Everything good?"

As soon as she stepped in her classroom, though, a crowd of former students greeted her with applause. The room had been decorated in her honor, and as she looked around she saw familiar faces, including a man who had been in the first class she'd taught 41 years earlier. She could hardly believe it: Everywhere she looked she saw familiar faces, now grown up. She recalled each and every one of their names. People doled out hugs; tears flowed freely.

Once in the room, former students had a chance to tell Ms. Flexer what she had meant to them. "You always wrote the sweetest notes in my report cards," one former student said. "You pushed me and my sister to do so well," said another, "and I think that's what makes you such a great teacher." Another recalled that "I was a timid little blonde, and your love for me gave me the confidence to grow into the woman I am today."

One teary-eyed student said, "I remember one particular day in school, for some reason you asked me to sing a song, and [after I sang] you got really excited and said, 'Oh, that's so wonderful. Go next door and sing for them.' So you had me walk around, to I think two or three different classrooms, singing this one song. For the first time I didn't feel awkward; I felt like something I could do was special."

Principal Chad High said that Ms. Flexer always "searched for what made each child unique and made sure she let each student know that they were special. She taught the same grade at the same school for 41 years. I don't know if I'd ever heard of someone staying at the same place that long, much less in the same grade."

"I'm one of the luckiest people in this world," Ms. Flexer said. "[This] was one of the coolest things that could've ever happened in my life. How many times do we really realize the lives we've touched, the manner in which we've touched them, and that these are memories that stay with them for life?"

Ms. Flexer began teaching when she was 21, and 41 years later, the importance of loving and cherishing each student who walked through her doors hit her. She was speechless. Former students presented her with a bouquet of flowers and a scrapbook to honor the occasion, and Kid President gave her a "Medal of Awesome." "My career could've taken me nowhere that would have made me happier. I think of it as a blessing," she said.

Who are teachers who have made an impact on your life? Tell them. You don't have to throw a big party (though we wouldn't discourage that). Just let them know they matter. Repay them in whatever way you can.

Former Cole Elementary School students return to celebrate their 1st-grade teacher, Ms. Flexer.

#87 TEACHERS keep teaching. STUDENTS keep Studenting.

Science. You're here. You take up space. You matter.

It's like Walt Whitman said, "YOLO." Except he didn't say that. You would know that if you'd read a book!

Everybody is a teacher, and everybody is a student. What are you teaching the world?

———

Right
We've been amazed at all the teachers and schools that have incorporated Kid President into their classrooms. We are convinced that if you want to change a community, it starts in a classroom. Thanks for teaching us that.

———

A quick chat with the former CEO of Chicago Public Schools and current U.S. Secretary of Education ARNE DUNCAN

What is your job as the Secretary of Education?
My job is to help the president make sure that every single student in this country has a chance to get a great education and follow their dreams. Some of the best schools in the world are in this country—but not every child has a chance to go to a great school. My job is to help more young people have that chance.

What made you want to do that?
When I was growing up in Chicago, a lot of my friends came from some pretty difficult neighborhoods. Some of them got a really good education—and some of them didn't. And their lives turned out really differently. I saw firsthand how much power education has.

Who was one of your favorite teachers when you were in school?
I've had so many great teachers! My English teacher in high school, Mrs. McCampbell, is one I will always remember. I've always written in blue ink—I still do, and a lot of the papers I wrote for Mrs. McCampbell came back with a lot of red ink on them. Sometimes that was hard to take, but I always learned from her feedback and it helped me become a better writer. She brought out the best in me.

How can schools make the world more awesome?
School is the place where you learn about possibilities—of where you could go, what you could know, what you could do, who you could be. Believe me, when I was a short kid in Chicago, I never thought I would be a pro basketball player in Australia, or that I would work for the president of the United States. Schools make the world awesome by opening everyone's horizons.

Lots of people who are still in school will read this book. Got any advice for them?
Absolutely. Here are four:
1. Go to college. No matter what. Let me quote Eric Schmidt, the guy who runs Google: "If all you care about is money, you should go to college. If all you care about is culture and creativity, you should go to college. If all you care about is having fun, you should go to college. Go to college."
2. At some point, someone will tell you there's something you can't do. Don't ever let their negativity pull you down. Instead, use it as fuel to work harder and pursue your passion. Prove them wrong not with your words, but with your actions.
3. The only thing you need to know is that you can learn anything.
4. You never know how the path you're on is going to curve, and when you'll come across someone again. Be nice.

Finish this sentence: The world would be more awesome if _____.
Every single child everywhere in the world had the chance to get an awesome education.

CHAPTER 9:
It's okay
to get
discouraged.
IT'S NOT OKAY
TO STOP.

#88 It's okay to GET Discouraged...

As you've seen, the road to awesome leads to some, well, awesome places. It isn't all cupcakes and kittens and kissing Beyoncé, though. Some days are hard. Real hard. You gotta keep going. Life is tough, but so are you.

People who give pep talks need pep talks, too.

When Robby had to have surgery to replace the rod in his left leg, it was a scary time. This was right in the middle of what was supposed to be a fun Christmas break. Robby always handles things with courage and smile, but the timing of this break was discouraging.

When our fans online found out about Robby's injury, he was flooded with support. Knowing that so many people cared made our family's holiday season a little brighter.

Sometimes, people who give pep talks need pep talks, too.

#89 ASK: "WHO DO I WANT TO BE?"

Grown-ups often ask kids: "What do you want to be when you grow up?" The answer they're looking for is some kind of professional career path. Answers like:

"I'm going to be a doctor."
"I'm going to build a spaceship and travel to Mars."
"I'm going to be a standup comedian who owns a crepes-and-corndogs stand on the side."

And it's an important question to think about. What you're going to be is a big part of your future. But even more important is the question: Who are you going to be?

JEFF FOXWORTHY has been a standup comedian and actor for 30 years, but that's not the only thing that defines him. He's a father. He works with children with cancer, and for the past 6 years, he has volunteered his time to serve the homeless. We asked Jeff about his work in the Atlanta homeless community and the importance of who you are.

Our professions can be important, but is that all that defines you?
I was doing an interview a month or so ago, and the lady who was interviewing me said, "So, you've been doing standup for 30 years. You've done TV shows. You've written books. Which one of those things are you?" And the answer is: All of those things are what I do—and I love what I do, I wouldn't want to do anything else—but that's not who I am. Who I am is a dad, a husband, a son, and a father. When we talk to kids, we always ask them what they want to be when they grow up. The answer that we are looking for is what type of occupation they are going to have. But all the different jobs you do doesn't change who you are. Who you are is what we all really need to work on.

So what do you do, and who are you?
What I do is I write jokes and make TV shows, but who I am is, hopefully, a compassionate man of character. If nobody is watching, I hope I will do the right thing, and if I have a choice, I will always err on the side of kindness.

And guess what? You can answer that question today. You don't have to wait until college or your first job to decide the kind of person you want to be. Some studies say that today's kids will change careers at least seven times during their lifetime. If that's the case, who you are becomes every bit as important as what you do because that's the thing that won't change.

So take some time and ask yourself:

WHO DO I WANT TO BE?

I really like that! So how does a person figure out who they're going to be?

I believe that we all have gifts, and it takes a while to figure out what those gifts are. But we all have those gifts. We can all make a difference. I tell my kids this all the time: when you look at other people who lead well-lived lives—who are the kinds of people you'd like to turn out to be—you'll find that every one of them cares about other people more than they care about themselves. They are not self-focused. And I think that's the truth. They have dropped their ego, and they think about others more than they think about themselves.

> ## "Always try to do your best, and always be kind."
>
> **Jeff Foxworthy**

It's not just about you, right?

At my house, we have a dry erase board that hangs on the wall going out into the garage. It has a message to my kids on it. It says: "It's not about you." I always try to tell my kids, "We only have two rules: 1) be kind, and 2) try." Always try to do your best, and always be kind. That's kind of my little mantra to live by. It probably sounds so hokey and corny and everything, but in my mind, good always beats bad. Kindness always beats evil. I think that's the convoluted message of spirituality. The part of spirituality that has gotten lost is that in loving on people, you are also the beneficiary of that. It changes you, and it changes every relationship that you have. And that can't be a bad thing.

Tell us a little bit about your work with the homeless and what you've learned from it.

A while ago, I met a guy who worked at a big homeless shelter in downtown Atlanta. He invited me down for lunch. I kept his card for years, and when I finally went, I was really moved by the stories I heard. I think that was a turning point for me—to realize that homeless people weren't different; they are just people like you and me. They got dealt some bad cards at one time, and they are struggling to get through that. So I started coming out to the Atlanta Mission on Tuesdays to run a group, and we're still doing it 6 years later. To see these guys work through some of the pain of their lives and finally get to the point where they can deal with it and make amends, it's just one of the most rewarding things I've ever done. It made me realize, everybody wants to be loved, everybody wants to be significant. And so when you look at people through that lens, it kind of changes everything.

Finish this sentence: The world would be more awesome if _____.

People thought of themselves less and of others more.

#90 HELP SOMEONE PROPOSE

One day we received this email:

"My name is Tucker. I was wondering if I could receive a little help with a marriage proposal. My girlfriend Brooke and I, when we first began getting to know one another, oddly but awesomely began getting to know each other with the help of your videos. I am horrible at talking sometimes, and your videos were a fantastic way to break the ice. I was just curious to see if you could help me out again by making a video that would lead into me asking Brooke to marry me. I know you may not have time. But I thought I'd give it a shot. —Tucker"

Tucker needed our help! We were in the middle of shooting our television show. The next day we were supposed to be interviewing rock legend Gene Simmons from the band KISS. That's when it hit us: Why don't we see if Gene wanted to help us help Tucker? We were a bit nervous to ask him, but we did.

Not only was Gene Simmons excited to help, he thought a song would be the best way to really "wow" Tucker and Brooke. With Robby on the drums and Gene on bass, the two improvised a song about why Brooke should marry Tucker. It was weird and unexpected and kind of beautiful. We couldn't wait to respond to Tucker's email with this video.

He was ecstatic after the special day: *"Thank all of you SO MUCH! She didn't expect a thing! And tell KP to keep playing those drums! You guys are so awesome."*

We were honored Tucker invited us to be part of his special day. As it turns out, Gene was honored we invited him to join in. That's the thing about doing awesome stuff. It becomes contagious.

P.S. In case you were wondering, Brooke said "Yes." Guess she was happy to be invited into Tucker's adventure, too.

91

Need some inspiration?
This is an inspiring page of inspiring things.

Call a friend!   Send a pep talk to yourself!   Get out there!

Listen to the *E.T.* soundtrack while riding your bike!

Blast music!   Popsicles!   Take a nap!   Draw a picture!

Watch a great movie!   Run around your house!

Write down why you started being awesome in the first place.

Take a walk in somebody else's shoes! (Ask first and return the shoes afterwards, please.)

Play air guitar!   Write a letter to somebody who has inspired you!

Do whatever it takes to get yourself on the road to awesome!

#92
Remember: Things don't have to be the way they are

As you set out to do awesome things, it's important to learn from those who have come before you. **MARTIN LUTHER KING III** certainly knows a thing or two about leadership and working to make the world a better place. The second oldest child of Martin Luther King Jr. and Coretta Scott King, he is a man committed to serving people in need. We've had the honor of meeting him at the 50th anniversary of the March on Washington and of his father's "I Have a Dream" speech. He has been a huge source of encouragement to us and we were honored to have this conversation together and share it with you.

What does the word "leadership" mean to you?
Leadership starts in the back. Sometimes we look in the wrong places for true leadership. The best leaders are great followers.

How important is it for kids to learn from leaders who have come before us?
It's invaluable. It's important to understand that while times have changed there are so many lessons and principles that we can gain from leaders before us. We have to continue to do our research and then recognize and renew some of the lessons of the past.

What are some things we can all do today to honor the leaders who came before us?
I think one of the things we can all do is continue to carry a spirit of gratitude. Being thankful for the work that others have done before us. Another thing we can do is to continue to educate and equip ourselves with not just the knowledge, but the historical perspectives and lessons from our past. Remembering that many of us would not have been able to get where we are without the help and resilience of those leaders who came before us.

What are some things you learned from your father that you try to always remember?
1. To love myself. You really can't love others if you don't first love you.
2. I have a loving family, so I have to also understand the importance of loving my family.
3. It's important to have a love of our community.
4. The final thing is my faith. And that is love of self, love of family, love of community, and love of God.

My dream for the world is to continue to realize my father's dream and that dream is not yet realized. My dream is to see my daughter, Yolanda Renee, who is now 6, see my father's dream realized and come true in her lifetime, if not in mine. We've come a very long way and have made some strides, but still have so far to go.

What advice would you give to your 10-year-old self?
To know and understand that you are never too young to leave an indelible mark on the world.

What keeps you going when things aren't easy?
What keeps me going is the thought that my parents and so many others alongside them kept going when things were far worse for them—and far worse than anything most of us will ever experience in our lifetime. So, I find that the greatest way to keep going is to be grateful and mindful of what others sacrificed for us to be where we are.

What can kids do to change the world?
Kids can and are changing the world every day by continuing to be curious and by being innovators. Through innovation, creativity, and curiosity, young people can continue to change the world at lightning speed. People like you, Kid President, are changing the world by caring, having a tender conscious and by getting involved and contributing to the world in positive ways.

Finish this sentence: The world would be more awesome if _____ .
We had more peace.

Martin Luther King Jr.

Above
Martin Luther King III with his wife, Arndrea Walters, and daughter, Yolanda.

#93 TAKE CARE OF YOURSELF, SO YOU CAN TAKE CARE OF OTHERS

KID PRESIDENT: MICHELLE OBAMA INTERVIEW

We have a favorite First Lady. There, we said it. So when the amazing FLOTUS **Michelle Obama** agreed to let us interview her, well, we kind of freaked out. Here is what she taught us.

Whoa, you have a can phone? How did you get one?
Oh, c'mon, Kid President. I've got my Twitter, my Instagram, so obviously, I have a can phone, right?

Obviously you have a can phone. And you called at the perfect time! I really need some help! I'm trying to figure out what the kids need to know. What are some of your favorite memories of being a kid?
Well, one of my favorite memories of being a kid was playing outside with my brother. We used to play softball. My dad taught me how to box.

Oh, box. Cool.
So we were a very active family. And I love spending time with my family doing great things outside.

Above Left
First Lady Michelle Obama uses her official tin can telephone to talk with Kid President in the White House Map Room. (Photo by Chuck Kennedy)

Opposite
Kid President takes a dance break with First Lady Michelle Obama.

> **"I think there are lots of things kids need to know, starting with how important it is to be active every single day and to eat healthy."**
>
> Michelle Obama

How can kids and grown-ups work together to change the world?
That's a great question. There are so many things that kids and grown-ups can do to save the world together because kids are really cool!

Kids are pretty cool!
They really play a big role in almost everything that I do here at the White House and across the country. Kids are an important resource for me and for the president. We want to hear their input and their ideas. So the first thing I want kids to do is speak up and to not be afraid to use their voices because people like us in important places need to hear those voices.

I can't believe you're listening to me. This is amazing. Thank you thank you thank you so much! You're my favorite First Lady!
Aw, thank you so much. You're my favorite Kid President!

So now that we're friends . . . what do you think the kids need to know?
Well, I think there are a lot of things kids need to know, starting with how important it is to be active every single day and to eat healthy.

I totally agree with you! Staying active is important. One thing I do to stay active is to dance. Do you think you can dance with me?
Absolutely. Let's move!

Yeah! Let's move!

Dance Break!

What's your favorite dance?
Oh, my favorite dance? The pencil sharpener. (Does the pencil sharpener. See page 162.)

Thank you so much for talking to me, and thank you for all the great advice!
Well I loved dancing with you and I loved talking with you. You are an awesome, awesome kid.

See you, Mrs. Michelle Obama—you're awesome.

*This interview first appeared on our television show, Kid President: Declaration of Awesome, which airs on The Hub Network. Special thanks to the White House for helping us talk to FLOTUS about her Let's Move campaign.

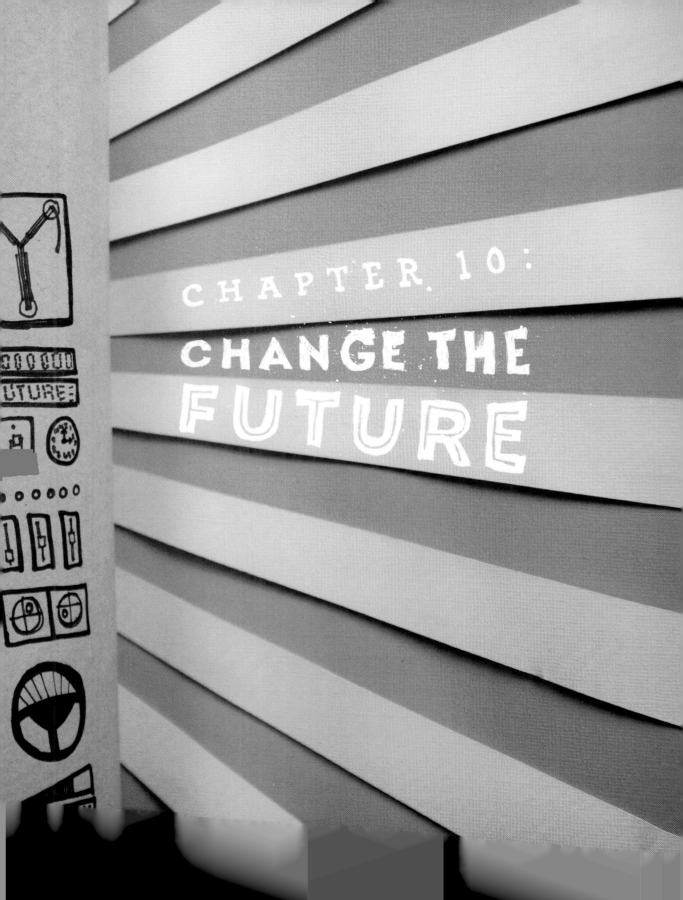

CHAPTER 10:
CHANGE THE
FUTURE

#94 CHANGE the FUTURE

Time travel doesn't exist, so we can't change the past. Good news, though! We can change the future! In fact, you're doing it right now.

It's important to look back so we can learn from the past. But it's equally important to look forward and think about how we can change the future. Take time to dream about how things should be and

#95 TEAM UP!

Together we're louder.

KEVIN OLUSOLA is a beatboxing cello player who performs with the group Pentatonix. Here, he shares his thoughts on collaboration, creativity, and making the world a better place through teamwork.

What's the secret to being awesome?
I think the secret is to find your passion and to do it with all your heart and soul. And to do it differently than others so you stand out from the pack!

How'd you learn to play the cello and beatbox? It's amazing.
I actually got the idea from my Chinese teacher the summer after my sophomore year when I was studying Chinese in Beijing. I started off doing simple things like scales over easy beatbox patterns, and it continuously grew from there! I would put up YouTube videos of myself doing this just to keep myself growing and to get feedback. And I'm still learning. On tour, I've been performing my first ever original piece for cello and beatbox! I'm hoping to continuously grow!

You're in the band Pentatonix with 4 other people. Is it hard to share the spotlight with them? Do you sometimes wish it were just you?
I really enjoy my time with Pentatonix! Being with them has made me realize that everyone does have their special talent, and that it doesn't necessarily mean that you're always in the spotlight. I think a lot of my talents come from the behind-the-scenes stuff, such as arranging, writing original songs, scheduling, business, etc. I love my role and am happy to do what I can to allow the band to succeed.

How can I be someone who collaborates better?
You have to develop a level of trust with your team so that you can openly and honestly express your opinions with the members. Also . . . leave your ego at the door! This about making something great with the team, and there's no "I" in "team"!

What would the world look like if more people acted like a team?
Well . . . we'd probably have a lot more happy people on this planet!

What inspires you to keep going?
I think knowing that there's so much I want to do in my life and I haven't reached my full potential yet keeps me going. I feel like there's so much more to who I am that haven't explored, so I'm excited for the journey ahead!

Finish this sentence: The world would be more awesome if _____.
Everyone could eat ice cream for lunch.

#96
Look ◄ BACKWARDS and FORWARDS ►

For a long time in the country of South Africa, there was a system called apartheid that kept white people separated from black people. Nelson Mandela wanted to change that, and he did. He eventually became the first black president of South Africa and ended apartheid. Nelson Mandela died in 2013, but his grandson **NDABA MANDELA** is keeping his grandfather's vision for a united Africa alive with his non-profit Africa Rising. He shared some of his wisdom with us.

What does it mean to be a leader?
A leader is someone who knows when to talk and when to listen, a person who is not threatened by people with great ideas but empowers those people and ideas.

How important is it to learn from leaders who have come before us?
It is very important to learn from leaders and former leaders. This will ensure that we don't make the same mistakes people have made in the past. If we are able to learn from their mistakes, we can make sure that we make new mistakes, which means that we will be closer to getting it right every time and truly making a positive difference in the world.

Shouldn't we focus on the future instead of the past?
We have to focus on creating a better future for our children and future generations to come. We have to try and make sure they get a world in good condition so they may experience some of the wonders and splendors the world has to offer, like wild life, rainforests, aquamarine life. To be able to breathe good, clean air, travel in safe, energy-efficient transport. We can do this by learning from our past and applying that knowledge today.

What are some things you learned from your grandfather?
I have learned the importance of legacy. Legacy is what will I be remembered for when I am no longer on this earth. What will people say about me? What will they associate my name with? I hope to be remembered for helping achieve the unification of our great continent of Africa and its people.

How can ordinary people live out extraordinary lives?
You can be an ordinary person doing amazing things for your community. That will make you larger than life and make you very valuable to the people in your community. Generosity puts a smile on one's face. It gives good, positive, warm feelings when one is generous to another. We learn to

appreciate each other as people, as human beings. It can go a long way in breaking down misconceptions of different groups, and it can even heal people.

Nelson Mandela

What are some problems in the world you'd like to see changed in your lifetime?
Racism is a big problem, and I hope one day this no longer exists. I want for people to realize that what separates black people and white people is not their skin color. For someone to be racist purely based on skin color is to behave like a caveman.

What's some of the best advice you've ever been given?
Always do what is right, and when you are not sure what that is, ask someone who loves you and believes in you.

What advice would you give to your 10-year-old self?
I would say it is very important to play team sports. And to believe in your dreams.

Finish this sentence: The world would be more awesome if _____.
We all love a little more.

#97 DREAM BIGGER

Who better to help us dream bigger than someone who has actually been to space? Meet our friend **RON GARAN**. He's an astronaut who has lived, worked, and walked in space. He's also served as an aquanaut doing research in Aquarius, the world's only undersea research laboratory. He's one of our heroes because he really believes that if we all work together we can create a better world.

When were you in space, and how long were you there?
I flew in space twice. I flew once in 2008 on space shuttle *Discovery* for a 2-week construction mission to the International Space Station. And then I flew again in 2011, launching from Kazakhstan on a Russian Soyuz rocket. We spent 5 and a half months on board the International Space Station on that mission.

When did you know you wanted to go to space? Was it when you were a kid?
Yeah, I was 7 years old, and that is without a doubt my most vivid childhood memory. It was my great-grandparents' 50th wedding anniversary, and my whole family was celebrating that. There was a black-and-white television there, and we all gathered around it and watched the *Apollo* moon landing. I wouldn't have been able to put it in words like this back then, but on some level, I realized that we had just become a different species. We were no longer confined to our Earth, and that really excited me. The exploration excited me. And for my whole life, from 7 years old on, that was what I wanted to do. I wanted to fly in space and explore and be an astronaut.

What did our planet look like from space? What was that like to see?
I think the big thing is the beauty. All the colors and the motion and the contrast is just indescribably beautiful. The only way I can describe it is to try to compare it to something we would see while we are on Earth, right? So you are sitting on a beach, and you're looking at this beautiful ocean scene. You can be amazed by the beauty and struck by the beauty of the scene, but you are anchored to that scene. You are connected to that scene via the sand, the ocean, and everything else. Gravity is pushing you down into that scene. When you see that beauty from space, you are completely detached from it. There's a vacuum of space separating you from the beauty. And the fact that you are floating and that this scene is either above or below you, depending on your perception, is a striking experience.

That's got to change the way you see things when you get back home, right?
There's an undeniable contradiction between the beauty of our planet and the unfortunate realities of life on our planet for a significant number of its inhabitants. That really hit me in the gut. Wouldn't it be wonderful if life on Earth was as beautiful as our planet was visibly beautiful from space? Was that wonderful for everybody?

That would be awesome.
I think the big thing we get out of the space program is that nothing is impossible. For thousands of

years, people would have thought it would have been impossible to fly to the moon and back. The space program and, most recently, the space station have proven that nothing is impossible. And if we work together . . . and that's where the International Space Station comes in. 15 nations worked together to build this incredible, most complex thing ever to be constructed in space. So if we could do that in space, imagine what we could do working together on the ground.

We can't all go to space, so what sorts of things can we do here on Earth to zoom out and have the same perspective that anything is possible?
To me, there is another aspect to this: something I call "elevated empathy." When I was in space, it was a lot easier for me to feel empathy for the struggles that all people face. When you fly over areas that you've never seen before, you start to go, "I wonder what life is like down there." You see the whole planet in a different light when you start doing that, and I think that can lead to "elevated empathy," where we look at the problems of someone on the other side of the world as our problems because we've panned back far enough that we could get everyone in the picture.

How can we do that?
I think the first thing is to put yourself in other people's shoes. I spend a lot of time talking about the framework that we tend to build to view the world through, and in that framework the world is a very, very complicated place. We have lots of problems. We have wars and conflict and crime and suffering and poverty, but we also have compassion and love and self-sacrifice and all that, too. Because of that complexity and the overwhelming nature of that complexity, a lot of people try to simplify things and try to put things into a framework or into cubby-holes. Unfortunately, when they do that, at times, they tend to put whole sets of people into those cubby-holes—whole countries, entire races. So what people can do every day is to try to take the time and make the effort to understand people. It's about putting yourself really, truly in other people's shoes before you judge them.

I would like to know how you think kids and grown-ups can work together to change things.
Kids have boundless energy; they have boundless curiosity, which leads to boundless creativity. They have not been taught what questions are not questions that you ask. They have not been taught where the box is, so kids naturally think outside the box because they haven't been put in the box yet. I think once grown-ups learn to respect this unbounded creativity and curiosity and bring children into the problem-solving process as partners—not as students to be instructed but as actual partners in the problem-solving process—I think that's the first step.

I think what we can do as adults would be to realize the respect that children really deserve. I think that's a global resource. We could tap into that childlike energy, that creativity, that curiosity. And the love, actually. Children have to learn how to hate; it's not something that is natural.
So, I think, children for the most part have a greater capacity to love, too.

Finish this sentence: The world would be more awesome if _____.
People could set aside their differences and learn to work together.

SPACE CAT

#98 WRITE DOWN YOUR DREAMS

We wrote it down jokingly: "Visit the White House."

While creating a list of ideas for videos we would create together, this idea came to us. For the big finale of our YouTube season, we thought it'd be cool if we actually got to go to the White House. Yeah, right.

It was a long shot. We never imagined it would even be a possibility, but we wrote it down anyway. Then, it happened. We've become very careful ever since about what we write down. We can't have just any dream coming true!

Now, just writing something down doesn't mean it will come true. We also wrote down some stuff about flying jetpacks (which has yet to happen). There is, however, great power in actually putting words together that say what you'd like to see happen.

Think about it. What are you dreaming of? What sorts of things would you like to see happen that could make the world more awesome? Write them down. Dream big, too. Your dreams make you who you are, so you should make them awesome.

A few excerpts from Kid President's Dream Journal - - - - - - - - - - - - - - →

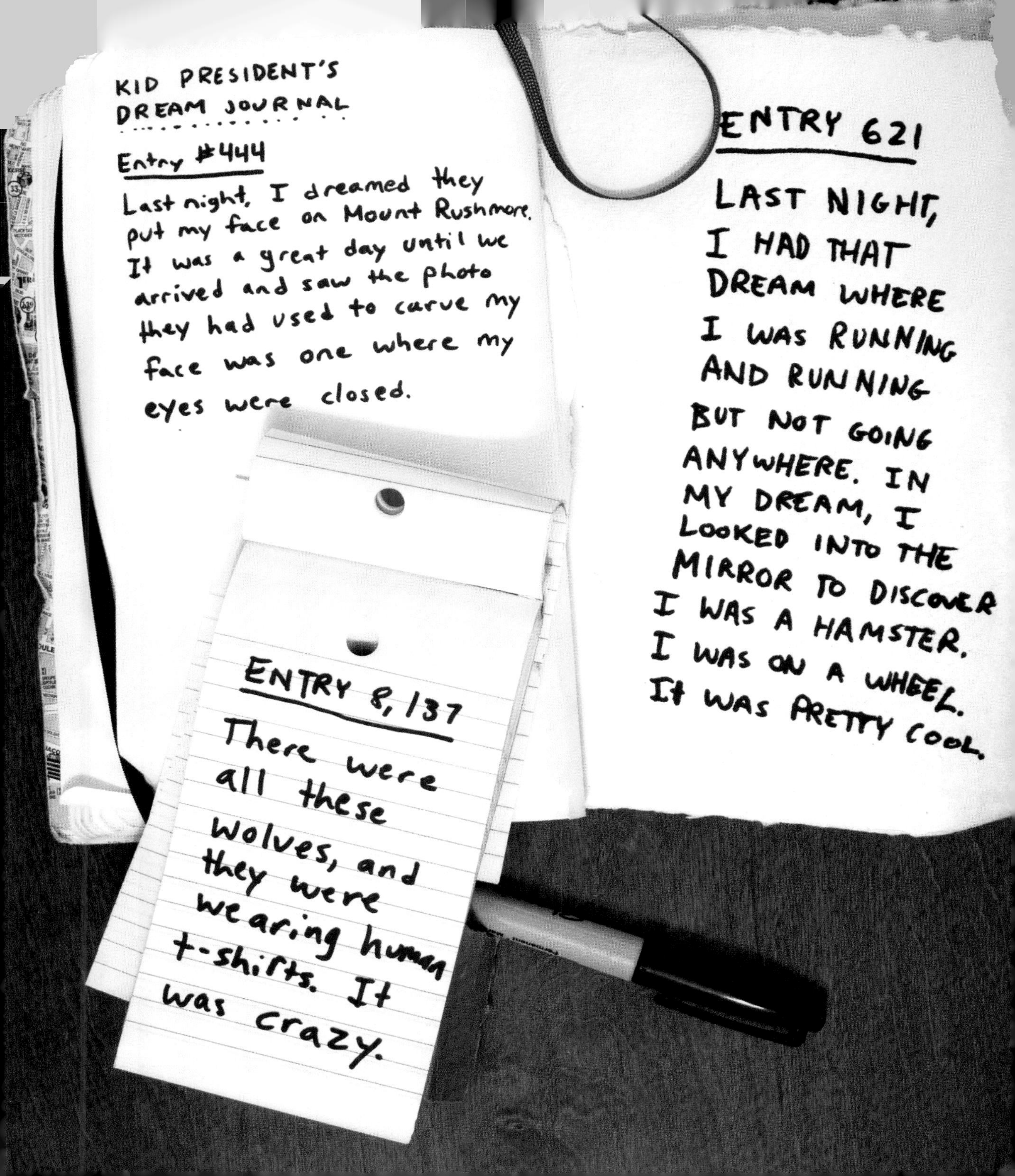

KID PRESIDENT'S
DREAM JOURNAL
....
Entry #444
Last night, I dreamed they
put my face on Mount Rushmore.
It was a great day until we
arrived and saw the photo
they had used to carve my
face was one where my
eyes were closed.

ENTRY 8,137
There were
all these
wolves, and
they were
wearing human
t-shirts. It
was crazy.

ENTRY 621
LAST NIGHT,
I HAD THAT
DREAM WHERE
I WAS RUNNING
AND RUNNING
BUT NOT GOING
ANYWHERE. IN
MY DREAM, I
LOOKED INTO THE
MIRROR TO DISCOVER
I WAS A HAMSTER.
I WAS ON A WHEEL.
IT WAS PRETTY COOL.

#99 REMEMBER THAT The World is BIGGER THAN YOUR Backyard

Take a moment to zoom out and look at the world differently. We're all on this planet together. We are on the same crew traveling through space on a giant spaceship called Earth. Let's act like it.

#100

Start writing on a page and then lose track of...

Okay, so we have to admit: We're tapped out of ideas. But that just means it's time for you to inject YOUR idea on how to make the world more awesome. Fill in this template, then cut it out to remind yourself everyday of your idea on how to make the world more awesome!

- ✂

What are you not okay with?

What do you have that can change that?

Who can you bring along to help you?

The world would be more awesome if _____.

Lean in close. We have something important to tell you. Are you reading closely? Great. Here goes:

Go be awesome.

There. We said it.

We know. We know. You don't need us to tell you. You can just go be awesome no matter what. You don't need permission or a hall pass or a special ticket, but just in case you thought you needed it—there it is.

You always have a choice. You could tone it down and be less awesome than you were made to be. You could completely shut yourself off from the world and do absolutely nothing. You could sit back and complain. OR you could be who we know you really are.

You might be thinking you should wait. After all, there is a lot of work that goes into being awesome. You already have a lot going on, too. It's not like you aren't doing anything. You're in the middle of trying to finish a book right now. It's a weird book, too. It's like the book knows exactly what you're doing. It's like it is talking directly to you.

Maybe that's because it is.

So, in case you've been waiting, here it is again:

Go be awesome.

It's time. You're ready to show the world what it looks like to be a party. The world needs more awesome. The world needs more of you. It needs people like you who care enough to fill it with more dancing and more love and more corndogs and more music and more light and more life. And that's exactly what you're going to do.

Go. The time to be awesome is now.

This book is almost over, but your adventure is just beginning.

I don't like goodbyes, but sometimes you have to say goodbye. Say goodbye to boring. Say goodbye to apathy—that means not caring about stuff. Say goodbye to those weird cut-off shorts. (Just figured you could while we're throwing stuff out.) Say goodbye to all the boring stuff, so you can start saying "Hello" to all the awesome stuff.

It's time to say "Hello" to possibility. Say "Hello" to hope. Say "Hello" to my cat, Shirley. Why? Look at her. She's so cool.

The greatest superpower we all have is the ability to change the future.
That's real talk.

Changing stuff can be hard, but we gotta do it. Especially our pants.
You gotta change your pants.

You might not think you can change anything, but you can. You will.
Just by being you.

Some days it'll seem tough. It'll seem like you're not getting anywhere. But every single day, you are adding a note to what adds up to be a big piece of music. Other people are making music, too. Together, we're all making a big song. And it's a really good song.

It's the kind of song that makes you want to dance and reminds you why dancing is awesome in the first place. We forget about dancing too much.

We forget a lot of important stuff sometimes. Birthdays. Responsibililiities.
How to spell "responsibilities." (I think that's it.) Worst of all—we forget that
if we want to be awesome, we have to treat people awesome.
Treat people like they are people, people.

If we all do that, we'll have a bunch of happy people.

Maybe you've been waiting for somebody to say this, so I'll say it: It's okay. You can go be awesome. Seriously. Go be awesome. The world needs more little notes adding to the music.

It's time. Play on.

KP out.

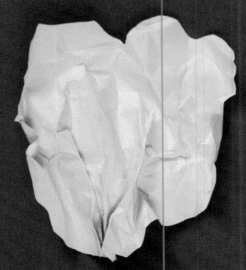

Life Is Like a
Really Good Sandwich.
FILL IT WITH THE GOOD STUFF.

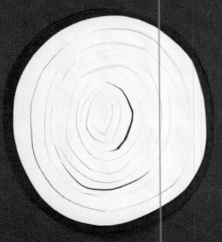

SURPRISE! IT'S A BONUS CHAPTER!

We know, we know. We were making you think this was the end of the book, and it was time to say good-bye, but now here we are in a bonus chapter! Feels great, doesn't it? It's like when you're eating a sandwich, and you think you've finished it, and you're a little sad, but then you look down and realize you dropped a whole bunch in your lap. There's still more sandwich! Hooray!

You may be asking, What sort of sandwich is this? Well, it's up to you! You see, life is like a sandwich—it's all in how you make it. You can fill your sandwich with anything you want. There are different breads, meats, cheeses, and syrups (who says sandwiches can't be sweet?). You can make your sandwich boring, or you can make it awesome. You can have it taste and smell any way you want. But if you want it to be tasty, you have to fill it with the good stuff.

Let's fill our lives with the good stuff.

But what is the good stuff? Well, we already filled this book with 100 awesome ideas for a good start, but we know you're hungry for more. You're not just anybody. You're on a quest to be truly awesome. If you really are ready to dive deeper, we'd like to share 10 more awesome ideas with you.

Thanks for going on this journey with us, friend. You make our sandwiches (and our lives) taste-tastic.

BRAD & ROBBY

#101 LIFE is like a REALLY GOOD SANDWICH.

FILL IT WITH THE GOOD STUFF.

#102 BE YOUR OWN BEYONCÉ

"Be yourself. Everyone else is already taken."

–Somebody really smart

Who is your hero? Who do you admire? Who do you look up to?

It's great to have heroes and role models. Sometimes, though, we can get so wrapped up in being just like our heroes that we forget to be who we are. Be you. You add something special to every single room you enter. The world needs the awesome that you have to offer. We need you to be you.

This doesn't mean you can't learn a thing or two from someone you admire. Take a look at the people you admire. Make a list of the things you look up to in them. Make a list of the things you'd do differently than them.

You'll soon find you have a voice of your own, and it's a good voice. You have a style of your own, and it's a great style. You have something awesome to share with the world. Be your own Beyoncé. We need you.

#103
CREATE YOUR OWN PRESIDENTIAL CABINET!

Did you know the president of the United States has a cabinet? It's a special group of people who help the president make decisions. (The cabinet is not a piece of furniture, though we have been to the White House and can confirm that it has many of those types of cabinets, too.*) Dating back to the first president of the United States, George Washington, there has always been a cabinet to assist and advise the president.

Surround yourself with wise people you trust to help you make awesome choices? Great idea! In fact, it's such a good idea, we decided to form our own cabinet. You can form one, too. Here are a few ideas:

Chief of Hats
This appointed officer will help you in all your hat decisions.

Secretary of Awesomeness
An executive officer appointed to make sure you only make decisions that are awesome.

Secretary of Cupcakes
A vital officer in your cabinet who makes certain you are equipped with cupcakes when you're sad, or even when you're not sad.

Secretary of Health and Whether or Not You've Been Showering
This officer is concerned with all your health matters. They let you know when your breath is bad, if you smell a little funny, or even if your pants are unzipped.

Note: You could also get a cabinet (piece of furniture). This might be useful for a variety of organizational needs, but do not ask furniture for life advice.

#104
· BE THE ·
COOL
TABLE

Too often in life there seems to be separation. Take lunchrooms as an example. Some lunchrooms are nothing but separation. There's a table for the athletic kids. There's a table for the band kids. There's a table for the kids who don't like tables. (It's a block of space where they can sit on the floor.)

In the lunchroom of life, don't let there be any separation. Be the cool table. Invite everybody to sit at it. Make it one big table where people, no matter how different they might be from you, can eat and laugh and have fun. Be the kind of table that welcomes all the other tables. That's a cool table. Let everybody around you know they're awesome. You're just that kind of table.

✂ -

PERMISSION SLIP FOR _____ TO BE AWESOME

This permission slip gives you and the people around you permission to be awesome.

Keep this in your pocket, give it to a friend, or save it for a rainy day.
It's just our way of helping you always remember: You were made to be awesome!

#105

Let BASS and TREBLE BE FRIENDS

People are different, and that's awesome. Sometimes, though, we forget that it's okay to be different. We can't have everybody all being the same. We need different.

We need bass and treble to be friends. The world just sounds better that way. A world with just bass wouldn't sound the same. We need bass. A world without treble wouldn't be the same. We need treble.

Help fill the world with music. When you disagree with someone because they're different, don't push them away. Be patient. Listen. Be thankful for what they add to the song.

#106
BE A SOLUTION.
DON'T BE A PROBLEM.

"We will be known by the problems we solve."
—Jeff Shinabarger (learn more about Jeff on page 169)

The world is full of problems, but it's also full of awesome people like you. We've loved hearing from and meeting so many problem solvers across the world. We're talking young and old and everywhere in between! It's incredible to see the difference one person can make.

There's no end to the solutions you can bring to the world! Start small. Start somehow. Just start! You'll be amazed at what good you can make happen. Here are some of the awesome people inspired by our book to be part of the solution!

How can you be a solution to a problem in your community?

ROSEMARY McKNIGHT is a 2nd-grade teacher in Tennessee who read about Christian's Buddy Bench (see page 120) and created one of her own!

Why did you start your own Buddy Bench?
I told the other 2nd-grade teachers about [the Buddy Bench], and we went in together and bought a concrete bench to put at the edge of a garden at our school. We shared the page about the Buddy Bench with all the classes and made the PE teachers aware of its purpose. Students were excited to have their own special place to go to when they are lonely, and they began to watch to see if someone was on the bench and try to include them in their play.

How else have you encouraged kindness in your classroom?
The Kid President book was released near the 100th Day of School. As part of our 100th Day of School celebration, I challenged the class to look for things their classmates did that made our class better. Students would take a strip [of paper] and write about the good thing they saw their classmate do, and we put it on a paper chain. I told them that when we got to 100 links, I would treat them to a party. They began looking for positive behaviors in each other and displaying more kindness. It was amazing how quickly we got to 100 links, and the students got a pizza party.

RICKY SMITH

Our friend Ricky is a writer and comedian who believes that random acts of kindness can make the world more awesome. So he started R.A.K.E. (check it out on social media by searching #RAKE). It stands for "Random Acts of Kindness Everywhere." Ricky took the concept of "pay it forward" and took it to social media! And it's more than an organization—it's an idea that changed the world! So we asked Ricky three important questions about kindness.

Why are random acts of kindness important?

Whether it's someone who is in need, someone who is a little down, or a complete stranger, kindness can brighten their day—the human connection is always there. I think we all get too wrapped up worrying about the small stuff (and 9 times out of 10 it's all small stuff), so when you can bring a smile to a complete stranger's face, it's amazing. To create a positive memory and experience for someone who isn't expecting it is beyond rewarding.

Can kindness really spread?

Absolutely! That's the power of social media. I saw people take my lead pretty quickly. My first documented #RAKE happened after I bombed an audition. Feeling sorry for myself, I was at a pizza shop and saw a bunch of homeless people out front. It immediately helped me put things into perspective. I bought a couple of pizzas and went outside and sat down and ate with my new friends. These people were so happy and grateful, but I think I got more out of it than they did! We took a selfie and posted it on Instagram. The next day, people in 7 other cities did the same thing and posted it online. The next day, another 23 people did the same thing, all posting with the hashtag #RAKE.

Do you have any tips for someone who wants to spread kindness?

Think small. You don't have to be rich or famous to do something for someone else. I always say, we all are going through something, whether anyone else knows it or not. So a kind word or gesture is always needed by all. But the thing I also say is, post it. Not to brag, but to motivate and inspire others to follow your lead and do something nice for someone else. The world needs more of that, especially right now. Imagine if everyone did one random act of kindness for someone else once a week how much more happy this world would be? Call me crazy, but I think we can actually come close to pulling it off.

Bonus question: What's your favorite dance move?

The running man!!! BEST DANCE EVER! It's awesome! It's a lot of movement, yet you are actually staying in place. Just doing it makes you smile! DO IT AND NOT SMILE, I DARE YOU!

(#110) IF YOU LOVE SOMETHING, share it!

#BookItForward

Part of filling our lives with the good stuff is doing what we can to fill the world with the good stuff! What's something you love that you want to share with the world?

When we were getting ready for our book to release, we thought it'd be fun to see what would happen if we invited people to share the stories they love. We called it "Book It Forward." The idea was simple: Give a book you love to someone you love. The responses made us dance!

Entire classrooms got involved. People left books in coffee shops with notes saying "Kid President told me to #BookItForward!" Others donated and distributed stacks and stacks of their favorite books to local libraries and shelters. We heard from people like **Rose Byrne** and **Quvenzhané Wallis**. We even

Opposite
Bottom
Quvenzhané Wallis and Rose Byrne share some of their favorite books with Kid President during an interview.

This Page
Above
Danie van der Westhuizen receiving a copy of the Kid President book from his friend Mathabo Baase.

Bottom Right
Sarah Ryan with some of the books she has collected with "Little Helpers."

heard from a new friend in South Africa named **Mathabo Baase**. She wrote in to tell us that she wanted to be part of #BookItForward by giving *Kid President's Guide to Being Awesome* to her friend for his birthday. (Top secret: She said she's in love with him and wanted to tell him as she gave him the book. Oh yeah!)

Our friend **Sarah Ryan** in Virginia is 9 years old. She was all about this idea way before we were. For the past two years, she's been leading the "Little Helpers Book Drive." She has collected over 2,200 books for her community. That's awesome.

You don't have to share this book. You can share any book. All the magical books and ideas and stories that have impacted you can have a big impact on other people, too. So we encourage you to find something you love (anything!) and share it! Good things happen when you spread good things.

CHECKLIST OF 100 AWESOME IDEAS

All of the ideas in this book are included below! We hope you'll give a few of them a try. If you do, please let us know! Email your pictures and experiences to kidpresident@soulpancake.com or tweet us @iamkidpresident. And if you want to suggest any new ideas for us to add to our list of 100 Awesome Ideas, let us know!

Just remember: Keep going, keep going, keep going!

Chapter 1: Life Is What Happens When You Put Down Your Phone (#1–#7)

- [ ] Put down your phone
- [ ] Take brain pictures
- [ ] Relax. Don't sweat the small stuff. Life is short and deodorant is expensive.
- [ ] Be less busy and be more awesome
- [ ] Let's live in a world with more high fives
- [ ] Bring awesome back (Justin Timberlake)
- [ ] If it doesn't make the world better, don't do it

Chapter 2: Focus on the Awesome (#8–#16)

- [ ] Focus on the awesome
- [ ] Look for what matters (Yash Gupta, Sight Learning)
- [ ] As human beings, we are capable of lots of bad stuff, but also cupcakes.
- [ ] Complain less. Celebrate more.
- [ ] Get out there! (Olivia Wilde)
- [ ] Every time you see a slide, go down it
- [ ] Sing out loud. You don't have to have a reason to.
- [ ] LAUGH! Help end global sadness.
- [ ] Follow your passion (Jack Andraka, teen inventor)

Chapter 3: Treat Everybody Like It's Their Birthday (#17–#28)

- [ ] Treat everybody like it's their birthday
- [ ] Mail your friend a corndog
- [ ] Have a pizza delivered to someone you disagree with (Bob Goff, U.S. Honorary Consul to Uganda)
- [ ] Every room you enter? FREE HUGS!
- [ ] If you see spinach (or anything else) in somebody's teeth, tell them, but only after you've told them something embarrassing about yourself
- [ ] We need to live in a world with fewer selfies and more otherpeoplies
- [ ] Practice the art of the unexpected burrito
- [ ] Recognize real beauty (Madison Hill, Miss Fabulous Pageant)

- [ ] Celebrate somebody's birthday by celebrating other people
- [ ] Two words: "Share"
- [ ] Sacrifice. Let someone else have the toy in the cereal.
- [ ] Be somebody who makes everybody feel like a somebody

Chapter 4: Talk Gooder! (#29–#36)

- [ ] Talk gooder
- [ ] Listen (more than you talk)
- [ ] Ask questions
- [ ] Stand in someone else's shoes (metaphorically) (Julia Stiles)
- [ ] Leave notes complimenting people on how well they parked
- [ ] Connect with people
- [ ] Ask people if they remember being a kid
- [ ] Make laughter your official language (Monique Coleman)

Chapter 5: Wanna Be a World Changer? Be a Day Maker! (#37–#56)

- [ ] If you want to be a world changer for people everywhere, be a day maker for the people right next to you
- [ ] Send a card. Every day. For 365 days.
- [ ] Be confident. It's contagious. (Nick Hornby)
- [ ] Find your light (and share it) (Josh Groban)
- [ ] Be cool to people even if they're not cool to you, because somebody was probably not cool to them
- [ ] Paint a park bench (Christian Bucks, the Buddy Bench)
- [ ] Ask your best friend for help (Catlyn Watkins and Addison Pointer, Handy Lunches)
- [ ] Invent a new handshake
- [ ] Solve a conflict using ice cream!
- [ ] Be fruitful (Katie Stagliano, Katie's Krops)
- [ ] Tip big, yo
- [ ] High five your dentist
- [ ] Declare an entire month something awesome! (Aaron Reddin, The One)
- [ ] Write letters (Sharon Li, We Care Act)
- [ ] Think more like a kid (Ryan Hreljac, Ryan's Well)
- [ ] Think of something you want to say, and then sing it instead (the Gregory Brothers)
- [ ] Write and record a song for someone
- [ ] Help somebody who is younger than you
- [ ] Read. Then read some more. (Adele Ann Taylor, Adele's Literacy Library)
- [ ] Love changes everything, so fill the world with it

Chapter 6: Be a Party! (#57–#73)

- ☐ Don't be in a party. Be a party.
- ☐ Be like cheese (or bacon) and make everything you touch better
- ☐ Throw a parade!
- ☐ Throw a pop-up art show (Bailey Hazouri, community worker)
- ☐ Take someone's photo and hand-deliver it to them (Jeremy Cowart, Help-Portrait)
- ☐ Give the world a reason to dance. (It's everybody's duty to do that.)
- ☐ Put tape on your nose. It's a great conversation starter.
- ☐ Come up with names for things that already have names
- ☐ Meow the words to your favorite songs. We call this cat caroling. (Craig Robinson)
- ☐ Behold the power of positive partying (Andrew W.K.)
- ☐ Spread confetti (the Earth-friendly kind)!
- ☐ Be kind. It's not always easy, but it's always important.
- ☐ Write a poem for somebody who doesn't normally get poems written about them
- ☐ Gather your friends, dress up like superheroes, and do someone's yard work
- ☐ Wear something awesome (Moziah Bridges, Mo's Bows)
- ☐ Invent a dance
- ☐ Join a movement!

Chapter 7: Make Something! (#74–#82)

- ☐ Make something awesome!
- ☐ Start with your heart and then just start (Vivienne Harr, Make a Stand)
- ☐ Be generous. Give! (Jeff Shinabarger, Gift Card Giver)
- ☐ Use your imagination! (Nirvan Mullick, Caine's Arcade)
- ☐ Spend time with your family! (Lennon and Maisy Stella)
- ☐ Broadcast the good news around you
- ☐ Start simple (Cassandra Lin, Project TGIF)
- ☐ Do what you like, and share it with others (Sam and Ben Tollison, A Monster to Love)
- ☐ Give out handmade awards

Chapter 8: Lick the Walls of the White House (#83–#87)

- ☐ Lick the walls of the White House
- ☐ Take a moment to reflect
- ☐ Kiss Beyoncé
- ☐ Let your heroes know they are your heroes
- ☐ Teachers keep teaching. Students keep studenting. (Arne Duncan)

Chapter 9: It's Okay to Get Discouraged. It's Not Okay to Stop. (#88–#93)

- ☐ It's okay to get discouraged . . .
- ☐ Ask: "Who do I want to be?" (Jeff Foxworthy)
- ☐ Help someone propose
- ☐ Don't get tired. Get inspired.
- ☐ Remember: Things don't have to be the way they are (Martin Luther King III)
- ☐ Take care of yourself, so you can take care of others (Michelle Obama)

Chapter 10: Change the Future (#94–#100)

- ☐ Change the future
- ☐ Team up! Together we're louder. (Kevin Olusola)
- ☐ Look backwards and forwards (Ndaba Mandela)
- ☐ Dream bigger (Ron Garan)
- ☐ Write down your dreams
- ☐ Remember that the world is bigger than your backyard
- ☐ Start writing on a page and then lose track of . . .

Bonus Chapter! Life Is Like a Really Good Sandwich. Fill It with the Good Stuff. (#101–#110)

- ☐ Life is like a really good sandwich. Fill it with the good stuff.
- ☐ Be your own Beyoncé
- ☐ Create your own presidential cabinet!
- ☐ Be the cool table
- ☐ Let bass and treble be friends
- ☐ Be a solution. Don't be a problem.
- ☐ Deal with the lemons
- ☐ Plant a tree!
- ☐ Throw kindness around like confetti!
- ☐ If you love something, share it!

acknowledgments

This book is the result of countless people who have loved us, believed in us, and supported us through Robby's 11 years and my 33 years. Thank you to our family for being the kind of family that dreams together, prays together, serves together, and makes sure things like this book happen together. To Russell Shaw, our amazing graphic designer, for bringing his many talents to this book through all the beautiful illustrations, hand-lettering, paper crafting, and loving care put into every detail you see here. To Rob Franks for keeping things on track and being the writer I wish I could be. To Irene Wang for being the only person who could create 47 different versions of the cover and still cheerfully respond to emails. To Bethany Eldridge for being a behind-the-scenes hero. To Katherine Leon for being a social media champ. To Young Chen for his kind words. To Cassidy Damore for his amazing laugh. To Bayan Joonam for seeing things we don't see. To Sarah North for her grace, grit, and goodness. To Katie England for her paper-sculpting skills but mostly her John Stamos macaroni art skills. To John Stamos for encouraging us all to have mercy. To Dave Coulier for encouraging us all to cut it out. Okay, no more *Full House* references—we have too many people to thank. Sorry. To the amazing Holley Seals-Lizarraga and her beautiful family for all of the cool props created for the TV show, which inspired us in a million different ways. Thank you to my 4th-grade teacher, Mrs. Debbie Perkins, and to Robby's 3rd-grade teacher, Mrs. Rosemary McKnight, for showing us what changing the world looks like by the way you lead your classrooms. To Matt Suggs for knowing when dudes who write pep talks need pep talks. To Matt Atnip for being Matt Atnip. To Erin Malone and the team at WME for teaching us how to behave in fancy offices. To the Montagues (Billy, Terresa, Matt) and Novaks (David, Laurie, April, Jeffrey, Alexia). To Ryan, Cayt, and Lily O'Neal; Matt van den Meiracker; Alicia Everett; and Zeke Lopez for all making our adventures worth having. To David Linker, Rebecca

Webster, Cindy Hamilton, Matt Schweitzer, Rick Farley, and all of our friends at HarperCollins for believing in this book. Big thank you to Devon Gundry, Golriz Lucina, Shabnam Mogharabi, and Rainn Wilson for dreaming up SoulPancake and creating a wonderful sandbox for us to play in. Special thank you to Shabnam, without whom nothing in the world would ever get done. To Bobby Miller, for believing in us when we only had 1,000 views on YouTube. To the dear Correy Stoner O'Neal for being an answer to our prayers. We love you like family. And to everyone who watched, shared, commented, emailed, liked, and helped spread this joyful rebellion in any way: Thank you.

Lastly, I must thank Kristi Montague. She is my wife, my friend, and art director for this book (and my life). If you found anything in this book or our videos worthwhile, it is because of her wonderful spirit. She inspired this project and every project I've ever taken on. She also receives credit for introducing me to one of my best friends ever, Robby Novak. He and I would like to dedicate this book to Miles (my son and his nephew) and our, as of the printing of this book, soon-to-be born little girl (my daughter and his niece).

BRAD

HOW WE WROTE THIS BOOK

The little dialogues throughout this book were pulled from actual audio recordings of conversations Robby and I had as we dreamed up what *Kid President's Guide to Being Awesome* would become. This book was created using the same process for how I write and produce our online videos. Robby and I eat food together. We laugh. We joke. We dream. We discuss. Sparked by our time together, I then pull together a script (or in this case, a book) that hopefully reflects the best of what we'd both like to share with the world.

PHOTO AND ILLUSTRATION CREDITS
Cover design by Russell Shaw and Irene Wang.
Paper art created by Kristi Montague, Russell Shaw, Katie England, and Bethany Eldridge.
All photos by Kristi Montague. All illustrations by Russell Shaw.
(Unless otherwise noted.)

4	Illustration by Brad Montague
13	Middle photo by Laurie Novak
17	Middle and bottom photos by David Novak
19	Illustrations by Brad Montague
39	Screenshots courtesy SoulPancake
42–43	Screenshots courtesy SoulPancake
50–51	Photos by Brad Montague
60	Photo courtesy Yash Gupta
63	Photo by Brantley Gutierrez
67	Photo by Mark Tucker
70	Screenshot courtesy SoulPancake
73	Photos by Golriz Lucina and Katherine Leon
75	Photo by Davis Goslin
76	Photos by Golriz Lucina
82	Photos by Robby Novak
84–85	Photos by Zach and Sarah Photography
86	Photos by Matt Atnip
87	Photos courtesy Zach Vanderslice
103	Bottom photo by Laurie Novak
106	Photo by Harry Fellows
110	Photo by Terresa Montague
111	Photo by Capra Photography
117	Photo by Lucy McNabb
118	Photo by James Dimmock
120	Photo by Alyson Bucks
121	Photo courtesy Catlyn Watkins
124	Photo courtesy Katie Stagliano
128	Photo by Jacob Slaton Photography
130	Photo courtesy the Li family
131	Photo courtesy Ryan Hreljac
132	Photo by Denny Renshaw
136	Photo courtesy *Lip Gloss* magazine
147	Photos by Jeremy Cowart

A TINY POEM

We dedicate this poem to kids and grown-ups everywhere who
are trying to make the world more awesome.

"Keep going. Keep going. Keep going."

The world is so big,
and we're all so small.
Sometimes it feels like
we can't do anything at all.
But the world can be better
(in spite of its flaws).
The world can be better,
and you'll be the cause.

Even though the waves
are bigger than our boats . . .
the wind keeps us sailing;
its love gives us hope.
Some days it's dark,
but we'll keep on rowing,
because people like you whisper,
"Keep going, keep going, keep going."